Krampus the Beast of Christmas
& Other Similar Beings

By the Family Kim

Krampus the Beast of Christmas

& Other Similar Beings

Written by the Family Kim

Illustrated & Edited by N. Kim & using public domain/open source images

Front & Back cover images – own creation using public domain/open source images

The Family Kim
Krampus the Beast of Christmas & Other Similar Beings
ISBN: 978-1-7637546-7-6

About the Authors

For more information about the authors go to the website:

https://www.seeingbeingsisbelieving.com/about-us-1

Table of Contents:

Everything About Krampus

Before the beginnings of Christmas or Halloween, there was a festivity that combined the two, it was called Samhain, followed by the belief in Krampus or similar known creatures. The pagan people celebrated Samhain. Samhain was later changed to Halloween, sometime in the 18th century. Samhain was outlawed during those times, because of the Catholic church. The old Christmas folklore and Samhain as it is known today was not around that time frame, similar festivities may have taken place in secret.

Since the 1700s, every year in early December (Krampus & other similar creatures that existed a long time before the belief in St. Nicholas, he/they are also known as the first Christmas beings), children in Austria (and the whole alpine region of Germany & Switzerland) would get ready for St. Nicholas to visit them. If they've been good, he'll reward them with presents and treats. But if they've been bad, they'll get a lot more than a lump of coal— they'll have to face Krampus.

6. December

Who's Krampus, you ask? He's the half-man, half-goat who comes around every year to chase naughty children and maybe even drag them to hell. European versions of St. Nicholas have long had scary counterparts like Belsnickle and Knecht Ruprecht who dole out punishment. Krampus is one such character who comes from folklore in Austria's Alpine region (and the whole alpine region of Germany & Switzerland), where he's been frightening children and amusing adults for hundreds of years.

Krampus and St. Nick's other bad boys (e.g. Knecht Ruprecht & many others) have their origins in pagan celebrations of the winter solstice. Later, some became part of Christian traditions in which St. Nicholas and Krampus visited children to reward/punish

them on the night of the 5th and 6th of December. In Alpine Austria and some parts of Germany, this day was known as *Krampusnacht*, or "Krampus night," when adults might dress up as Krampus to frighten children at their homes.

Children might have also seen Krampus running through the streets during a *Krampuslauf* – literally, a "Krampus run." If Krampusnacht was a way to scare kids into behaving themselves, the Krampuslauf, which isn't tied to a specific day, was a way for grown men to blow off steam while probably still scaring kids. Men would get drunk and run through the streets dressed as the fearsome creature. Like Krampusnacht, the Krampuslauf tradition continues to the present day.

The introduction of mass visual media couldn't help but sweep the charismatic Krampus up in its wave. When the postcard industry experienced a boom in Germany and Austria in the 1890s, it opened the way for *Krampuskarten*
.

These holiday cards weren't mean to make you feel warm and fuzzy. Ones marked "Gruss vom Krampus" ("Greetings from Krampus") showed Krampus stuffing a distressed child into his satchel or preparing to hit one with his bundle of birch-sticks. Many of these postcards depicted Krampus going after children with his sticks, leading them away in chains, or carrying them off in his bag.

There were also cards that were a little more...adult. Krampus cards in the early 20th century show him punishing children, yes, but also proposing to women. In some cards, Krampus is portrayed as a large woman whipping tiny men with her birch sticks and carrying them off in her satchel. In another, a smiling woman dangles a defeated-looking Krampus in the air, holding his

bundle of birch sticks behind her back. You can draw your own conclusions about the gender politics in these.

For over a century, people of the world probably never saw a Krampus card or even knew who Krampus was. That changed in 2004, when art director and graphic designer Monte Beauchamp published a book of Krampus cards and helped to organise an art show inspired by the cards.

Whether or not Beauchamp is primarily responsible for introducing Krampus cards to the new world. Krampus has since become a sort of ironic icon everywhere. Etsy has a whole section of items inspired by classic Krampus cards. And if you don't have time to send cards, you can buy an ugly Krampus sweater to wear to your local Krampus party or Krampuslauf. Krampus' popularity in the world arguably peaked with the 2015 feature film *Krampus*, which shouldn't be confused with the many other low-budget Krampus movies. Although Krampus is relatively new to the world, this alpine legend is the original bad Santa.

Stories About Krampus

A Krampus Story

Stefan opened his eyes, and he realised his body was cramped. He tried to move, but found that he was inside some sort of a rough canvas bag that scratched at his face and hands and feet. Sure that it was a bad dream, Stefan pinched his cheeks hard, but just yelped in pain.

He wasn't dreaming.

The last thing Stefan remembered was falling asleep in his bed. It had been Christmas Eve, and he was anxiously awaiting finally getting his first car. Even though he was a few years away from being able to legally drive, his sister had also gotten her first Porsche at 13, so he was sure he'd get one this year as well.

Thoughts of his new car vanished as he brought himself into the present. He had no idea how he had gotten into this rough sack, but he knew that he had been kidnapped. Stefan thought about his classmate Donald who had gotten kidnapped when he was vacationing in South America. He had thought it would be cool to be kidnapped, as you were only kidnapped if your parents were super wealthy or famous, but this was not cool at all.

Stefan tried to call for help, but there was no response. He struggled a bit, and as he pushed against the burlap sack, he could suddenly feel fresh air on his shoulder. Stefan curled up his body and tried to reposition himself so he could press against the small hole with his fist.

After managing to get his hand free, Stefan felt around and grasped a long piece of cord. He tugged at it, and after some time, the knot fell away and the bag opened up. The walls of the bag fell around Stefan's body, and he suddenly felt scared, as he was no longer obscured in his sack.

Even though Stefan was dressed in his Gucci tracksuit he wore as pyjamas & a skull ring he wore on his finger, he felt alone and naked, as he realised he was definitely not in a good place. The floor was made of cobblestones, and the only light came from a series of torches mounted on the wall. The stone walls were covered in black filth, and there were chains and shackles hanging from them. Mounds of dirty children's pyjamas and slippers littered the area, and across from where Stefan stood, it looked like a butcher shop out of a horror film.

Chunks of meat hung from hooks, and a collection of large knives hung on the wall above a sink. Stefan didn't realised that the handles of the knives were all repurposed bones, but he didn't need to in order to realise he needed to get out of there.

He slunk past a giant bubbling cauldron so large he would have to tiptoe to even have a chance of seeing into it, but he looked back at all of the kid-sized slippers littering the place, and didn't want to know what was being cooked. Stefan tried to step quietly as he moved through the cavernous space, sticking close to the walls. There were not many hiding places, but the shadows cast by the pillars along the walls were deep enough that he might hope to be overlooked by anyone coming his way.

As he came upon a doorway, Stefan froze. There was a narrow spiral staircase of stone steps leading upwards. Realising there would be no place to hide, and having no idea how long the staircase went, Stefan weighed his options. If he stayed, a bloody death at the hands of some unknown monster was certain. If he fled, he might get caught again, but at least there was a chance he might be able to escape before he was found.

Stefan took a deep breath to calm himself, and then began to ascend the stairs. The stone steps quickly became cool as he climbed, the heat of the kitchen fading quickly as he rounded the first bend. Stefan looked up, and all he could see were more stairs and darkness. There were no torches on the walls here. Stefan's heart felt like it was going to burst through his chest, but he knew he had to continue on.

Step by step, Stefan climbed the stone staircase, and his eyes began to adjust to the darkness the best they could. The stairs were so devoid of light, he could barely make out the next step, so he clung to the wall and moved carefully. He looked down, then up, and there was no telling how long the staircase went on, or how far he had come. Stefan sighed, but continued on.

Stefan had no idea how long he had been climbing the staircase. He hadn't counted each step, and with no way of knowing if he was close to the top or how far he had come, time had slipped away. His legs began to hurt, and his feet were almost numb, as the steps had grown icy cold quite a long time ago. Stefan had been sweating when he left the dungeon-like kitchen, but that sweat had cooled and dried, and now he found himself shivering.

Suddenly, he could see a faint glow coming from above, and a radiant warmth became apparent. Stefan's steps were painful, but he forced himself up quicker now, as the allure of the heat overrode his caution.

The higher he climbed, Stefan could feel the chill fade away, and he wasn't sure if he was hallucinating, but he could swear he smelled hot cocoa. Where was he?

Stefan followed the warmth and light and had to squint his eyes as the light became stronger. The young boy paused where he was, letting his eyes adjust to the light again after being so long in the dark. The stone steps were warm again, and he dropped down to crawl those last few steps. The staircase felt warm, and Stefan had half a mind to fall asleep there, cradled by its warmth after his long, frigid trek.

Stefan slowly pulled his weary body up, step by step, and he peeked out from the mouth of the staircase. He saw a great hall filled with Christmas lights strung up along the high beams leading to the most massive Christmas tree Stefan had ever seen. It was covered in glistening blown glass ornaments and shimmering tinsel. The tree towered above all of the small, unattended child-sized workbenches and stools that sat in neat little rows. Along the walls were a plethora of giant fireplaces, all spaced apart so that the heat could be felt even from where Stefan stood.

Stefan looked around hesitantly, this new environment so different from the cold, brutal underground he had emerged from. The great hall was empty, and so he tentatively stepped out towards the nearest fireplace and took a seat.

The heat warmed his frigid body, and he slowly began to stop shaking. The feeling returned to his fingers and toes. The warmth felt so good, Stefan could barely keep his eyes open. Cradled by the heat, he wrapped his arms around his knees and felt his eyes begin to close.

'Hey there, friend,' a strange voice said.

Stefan's eyes shot open and he yelped as he spun around. Stefan saw a tall man with a kind face smiling at him.

'Sorry to scare you, I forgot something in the workshop so I came back to get it, but then I found you and I just thought you looked lost and could use some help,' the tall man stated.

The man was thin but muscular, and was wearing a forest-green vest and red pants. He looked young, but somehow seemed much, much older.

'Are you okay?' the tall man asked Stefan.
'Uh, where am I? Who are you?' Stefan asked unsure of where he now found himself.
'Well, you're at the North Pole at Santa's Workshop! My name is Rudolph, but you can just call me Rudi,' Rudi spoke plainly and extended his hand outward, Stefan tentatively shook it.

Rudi's hand was smooth as silk.

'Hi Rudi, I'm Stefan. Stefan Benson,' Stefan replied quietly.

Rudi smiled then said, 'Hello Stefan Benson. You seem quite a far way from home. I know not of any human families living nearby.'

A confused look came over Stefan's face.

'Ah, I am an elf, Stefan. As are almost all of the resident craftspeople here at Santa's Workshop,' Rudi said in a jolly voice.

'But, you look human. And elves and Santa don't exist,' Stefan stated sceptically.

'Ah, Stefan, you see, I most certainly am an elf, and I'm here in flesh and blood right before you,' Rudi said and brushed back his long silver hair to allow a giant, pointed ear to extend from its hiding place.

'Also, Santa is most definitely also real. I know it seems like he isn't, but it serves our purposes much more easily if most people don't believe it's so,' Rudi stated defiantly.

Stefan wasn't sure what to believe anymore. Was he really at the North Pole?

'Stefan, I'm sure all of this is a lot to take in, but let me show you something,' Rudi stated trying to reassure Stefan.

Rudi walked over to the stone wall next to the fireplace, and pressed his hands against the stone. The stone gave way as if it was made of liquid, and Rudi muttered something as he pulled his hands outward. The wall seemed to stretch as as newly formed window, complete with ornate grilles joining the multiple panes of glass, seemed to appear out of nowhere.

Stefan gasped as he slowly walked over. He slowly reached out and touched the icy glass. He tried make out some sort of buildings or signs of life, but all he could see was a world of swirling white snow and far off mountains of ice.

'Whoa, how did you do that?' Stefan asked as he stared at the window, then at Rudi, then back to the window.

Stefan pressed at the sill, the polished rock smooth under his hand.

'It's magic, Stefan. Craftsman magic, to be precise. It allows a skilled user to create new things out of old, like a new window where none was before. Or it allows us to make toys for the good little children around the world,' Rudi tried to explain, then smiled beaming with pride.

'Wow,' Stefan said, smirked and stepped back.

'What else can you make? Can you make me a drone? Or a laptop?' Stefan said in a selfish tone.

Rudi chuckled: 'Slow down, my little friend. Before we get carried away here, we really should be getting you back home. Your parents are going to miss you.'

'Can your magic do that, Rudi? Can you make me a door that'll transport me back home to Illinois? Or can you make a teleporter gun that'll make a portal that'll get me back home?' Stefan asked out of curiosity.

'I'm a crafts person, Stefan, not some wizard,' Rudi explained.

Stefan frowned at this remark.

'My magic isn't nearly strong enough. I'm only 800 years old. In order to even attempt transcontinental teleportation, I'd need to be a few centuries old. But there is someone who can easily fold space and time, and that's Santa himself,' Rudi stated calmly.

Stefan smiled: 'So there's a way to get back home?'

Rudi shouted gleefully, 'Definitely! I'm not even sure how you got here, but whatever happened, I'm sure Santa will be able to take you back to where you belong!'

Rudi beamed a huge smile and then spoke, 'Why don't we head over to Santa's room and meet him now?'

The horrors of being woken up in the sack and the piles of children's clothes suddenly came back to Stefan.

'Wait, I was kidnapped! I woke up in some sack downstairs!' Stefan stepped backwards, suddenly suspicious of his new friend.

'Ah, Stefan, I understand. The caverns below this workshop belong to Krampus - think of him as Santa's counterpart who deals with naughty children. He kidnaps children and brings them here to scare them, then leaves Santa to take them back to their homes,' Rudi explained trying to calm down his new friend.

'But, I saw a bunch of kids' pyjamas and slippers in a pile down there! I've read the stories - he's eating them!' Stefan shouted.

Rudi laughed: 'Oh, Stefan, don't be silly. Those are the discarded clothes that the children have left behind after they've gotten their new holiday outfits from Santa. And yes, Krampus is also our chef who catches and butchers seals and fish and sometimes the occasional killer whale. As I remember, dinner should be served soon, and I think seal stew is on the menu. He doesn't ever eat children - his scary visage and mythology is just to frighten them into behaving better.'

Rudi smiled his warm smile again, and Stefan couldn't see any hint of lying. It did make a lot more sense. After all, if Krampus was really going to eat him, would he have really just left Stefan to escape?

Stefan smiled, and Rudi took Stefan's small hand in his own.

'Let's go meet Santa, shall we?' Rudi said and led the way through the joyous halls to a large red door, decorated with a beautifully lush wreath.

Rudi knocked at the door and spoke, 'Santa, may I request an audience? I have found a lost child, one of Krampus's abductees, I presume.'

The door creaked open.
Rudi walked in, but Stefan hesitated.

Rudi looked back at the cowering boy and said, 'Don't worry, Stefan, Santa will make things right! He'll take you home, come on!'

Stefan slowly released his grip on the door and walked into the room. The room was sparse, surprisingly so given the level of decoration in the grant hall. There were giant fur rugs on the ground, and a single fireplace that housed some glowing embers. Large candelabras floated in the air, suspended by some magical force, and in the far corner was a giant chair that looked almost like a throne. Stefan's eyes grew wide as he saw a giant, jolly-faced man dressed in a red robe with white furry trim seated there.
Rudi gently ushered Stefan forward.

The boy looked up at the massive man in front of him and said, 'Santa?'
'Ho, ho, ho, why hello, Stefan Benson. Welcome to the North Pole!' Santa shouted very loudly and let out a belly laugh, then smiled, his white teeth shining in the candlelight. 'I see our old boy Krampus has been up to no good,' Santa went on to say.

Santa stood, and walked over to the pair. Rudi was tall, at least six feet tall by Stefan's guess, but Santa towered over even Rudi. Santa was a giant, and Stefan understood why the door was so large.

'I found him in the workshop, sir, and thought you'd be able to bring him back to his home in Illinois, back in the United States,' Rudi replied to Santa.

'Ahh, thank you, Rudi, you did a great job. Also, good work on those stone fountains you created yesterday. Top notch masonry, and the electronics were well-done as well!' Santa praised Rudi.

'Thank you, sir, your praises are too kind,' Rudi beamed and bowed his head.

'Oh, Rudi, while I prepare little Stefan here for his trip back home, would you be a dear and gather up the rest of the elves? I believe it will be dinner time soon,' Santa said in a slightly menacing tone.

'My pleasure, Santa,' Rudi said naively, bowed deeply and turned to leave.

'Nice to meet you, Stefan. Have a safe trip back home!' Rudi said in a somewhat cheery tone to Stefan.

'Thank you, Rudi! Thank you for everything!' Stefan said in an unsure tone and waved to Rudi.

Rudi smiled, waved back, then turned and left.

Santa smiled, then waved his hand and the giant door slowly closed.

'Well, then, Stefan, let's get you back to where you belong, shall we?' Santa spoke, smiled, and waved his hand again, and a glowing blue portal appeared.

'Just head through that portal and you'll be back where you belong,' Santa explained to Stefan.

'Oh, uh, Rudi said something about new clothes as well?' Stefan stated quickly.

Santa looked at Stefan for a second, then smiled again and said, 'Ah yes, the new outfit. How could I have forgotten?'

Santa snapped his fingers, and a giant wrapped gift box appeared in front of Stefan.

'Why don't you try them on when you're on the other side?' Santa suggested to Stefan.

And with that, Santa pushed Stefan through the portal.

Stefan landed on a pile of warm laundry. But as he looked up at the ceiling, instead of his familiar blue ceiling, he saw moss-covered stone. He looked to his side, and realised he wasn't lying on a pile of laundry, but a pile of discarded pyjamas.

Stefan sat up, and sure enough, he was back in Krampus' kitchen. He realised that he was naked, his tracksuit crumpled next to him. The ceiling began to warp and twist, and Santa dropped down through the void. He walked next to the cauldron, picked up the giant ladle, and began stirring the pot.

Stefan asked in a scared tone, 'Santa?'

Santa stopped stirring the cauldron and walked over to where Stefan was cowering. Stefan noticed Santa had stopped smiling.

'That's my name when I'm up there,' Santa slyly spoke.
Santa's voice dropped a few registers as he spoke, his jovial tone turning into a bestial growl: 'But now, we're down here, right where you belong.'

Santa's jolly face began to drip off, and Stefan screamed. Stefan watched as as Santa's hair turned dark black and his eyes coal-red. Horns began to sprout, pushing back his red hood, as his lips seemed to fall off. Santa's teeth grew extended and sharp as a sickly, tongue fell from his mouth, lolling around like a worm.

Krampus stretched out his hand as one of the knives flew from its place above the sink into his hand. Stefan screamed again and didn't stop for a painfully long time.

——

Rudi spoke, 'Santa?'

Santa looked up from his table to see Rudi staring up at him, Santa spoke, 'Yes, what is it, Rudi?'

'I was wondering - if you dislike Krampus' methods of scaring children so much - why do you let him continue to do that? Any one of us elves could easily take over the cooking duties given proper training,' Rudi asked Santa contemplatively.

Santa smiled his jolly grin and spoke once more, 'Rudi, as distasteful as it is, Krampus' methods do wonders to make sure children are behaving. After all, he only kidnaps children who are so twisted and evil that they're beyond redemption.'

'Beyond redemption? But Santa, don't you take all of those children back to their parents after their fear of Krampus has inspired a new way of living?' Rudi said in a confused voice.

'Of course, good Rudi, of course. What I meant to say was that if Krampus never got involved, these children would never be able to stay on the true, righteous path we try to inspire with our gifts. For the hundreds of children who might be encouraged to be kind and generous through positive encouragement, there are always a few who must be encouraged to curb their wicked ways through fear. It is not the way I wish the world to be, but how it is. Just think as

Krampus as, well, someone who shares the same beliefs that I do, but just acts upon them in a different way,' Santa carefully explained.

'I see. But, what about Stefan? Was he really that bad?' Rudi asked Santa.

'To be honest, Stefan was not a good child. He bullied others and tormented many of his classmates. He had zero empathy for anyone but himself, and he was a manipulative, cruel little boy,' Santa replied in an annoyed tone.

'But, he seemed so nice,' Rudi said as his face contorted as he tried to reconcile the new information.

'Rudi, you haven't been out there to see the human world, but when they get in trouble, bullies are just like any other child. They cry, plead for help, rely on the kindness of strangers - but once they get an ounce of power, they start taking and taking and their greed and need for power consumes them,' Santa explained, trying to keep himself still.

Santa walked over to Rudi, put his hand on the elf's shoulder and spoke, 'I know your mind is troubled, Rudi, but go have another bowl of the stew, and think not of Krampus and his unsavoury methods or the evils of the world. Go eat up, son, and let the meat give you the strength to continue on the righteous path. Just focus on all of the good children you're helping through your work,' Santa said reassuringly.

'Thank you, sir. I appreciate your time and guidance,' Rudi said in a happy voice and with that, Rudi turned, walked back and filled his bowl with another serving of stew.

Make your own ending or continue reading below:

Rudi went to get another bowl of stew from the cauldron. Once he had his serving in his bowl, he was about to eat when he spotted something floating in his stew. An odd, round shaped, slimy thing was in his food. Until Rudi realised it was an eyeball, that was just sloshing around in his bowl. Rudi was disgusted as well as scared at the same time. Now the stew was more ew than anything. Rudi put the bowl on the table, as soon as he placed it down on the surface of the table, he saw a finger floating in the stew, a

finger that had a skull ring on it. Now it was obvious to Rudi that he had eaten bits & pieces of Stefan. The room was quiet, too quiet, even Rudi could notice this. However, he failed to notice a big, fat & plump shadow looming over him. Rudi turned and was greeted by something that looked like a combination of Krampus & Santa, with humongous, sharp & elongated white shiny teeth and monstrous looking eyes.

THE END

The Two Sisters & Krampus

Once, a long time ago, there were two sisters; one called Mary who was very, very good and one one called Emily who was very naughty.

And on one Christmas Eve, the Krampus; the goat headed monster that people say carries off naughty children, came down their chimney and stole away Emily in a sack, leaving behind a lump of coal to show that he had been there. But Mary loved her sister so much that when she saw that her sister was missing and when she noticed the lump of coal she started to cry.

When she saw the present that Santa Clause had left her under the tree she said, 'Whatever my present is, I do not want it. I would rather have my sister back.'

But then, to Mary's astonishment, she saw a label magically appear upon the present and when she read the label, it said, 'What is inside this present may help you save your sister.'

Mary, decided to tear open the present, inside she saw a golden pair of scissors, a candle of frankincense and a bottle of Myrrh. She picked up the scissors, the candle and the bottle and, immediately, she was transported to a dark coalmine, where she saw a chain gang of little children working with picks and shovels.

'Where is this place?' she asked one of the children, a little boy, who was digging with a pick.'
'This is the coalmine of Krampus where he makes naughty children dig coal,' said the child.
Mary told the little boy not to worry, that she had come to rescue all the children from Krampus and then she used the golden scissors to cut through the iron chains that bound the children as easily as if they were paper chains.

And, looking among the children, she found her sister Emily and hugged her, happy to be reunited reunited with her. Unfortunately, when Emily told her that the tunnels of Krampus's coal mine were like a labyrinth and only the beast knew the way out, Mary frowned.
Mary then for some reason lit the candle of Frankincense and, to all their amazement, the candle became a star, shining like the star of Bethlehem and, following the star along a maze of dark tunnels, Mary and the children found their way out of Krampus's coal mine. But then outside the entrance to the coalmine, they saw a room where Krampus was lying on a bed snoring, fast asleep.

'What are we to do now?' asked Emily.

Mary opened up the bottle of Myrrh.

'Myrrh is for anointing people with,' she said.
'So perhaps we are to anoint ourselves with it. And saying that she poured some on her hand and as soon as the fragrant oil touched her hand it became invisible.
'This must be to hide us from Krampus,' Mary said and proceeded to pour Myrrh over her head and the heads of Emily as well as the other children making them all invisible.

Then, being careful not to make any noise, the children tip toed across the room to the door of Krampus's house and, opening it went outside. Outside, they saw that they were on the top of a snowy mountain and there was no way down the mountain.

'We're trapped! How do we get home now?' said Emily.

Just then, however, they heard the sound of sleigh bells and then, across the sky, they saw Santa riding in his sleigh pulled by flying reindeers.

'Quick children,' said Santa Claus, landing upon the side of the mountain.
'Get on board my sleigh before Krampus catches you,' Santa said in a rushed tone.

And so Mary and the other children got onto the back of Santa's sleigh and then, tugging upon his reigns, Santa Claus made the sleigh rise up into the air and they flew off across sky.

'But Santa, why are you helping us? I thought that Krampus worked for you, to punish naughty children,' said Mary in a nervous voice.
'Don't believe everything you hear. Krampus is really my mortal enemy. Just as I was chosen by the powers of light to bring Christmas cheer to all the children of the world he was made by the powers of darkness to spoil Christmas,' said Santa Claus.

But then, suddenly, from behind them they heard the sound of howling and, turning round, Mary saw Krampus pursuing them in a sleigh drawn by a pack of flying arctic wolves. Then Krampus started to hurl lumps of coal at them.

'We're under attack,' said Emily as a coal lump went whizzing past them.

But then Mary picked up one of the parcels that were piled up in the back of Santa's sleigh.

'We can use these,' she said.

Then she and the other children started to throw the parcels at Krampus and Emily hit the old goat right between the horns so that he fell backwards off of his sleigh, plummeting to the ground far below. But then, as they were looking down, they saw Santa's workshop and, tugging upon the reigns, again, Santa Claus brought his flying sleigh in to land beside it. Then the doors of the workshop magically opened and they all followed Santa Claus inside. Mary and the other children saw all of Santa's little gnome helpers dancing and singing and having a Christmas party. The gnomes gave them all cake and ice cream to eat and lemonade to drink. Then they joined in the dancing and singing until they all started to feel very tired and Mary and Emily were sitting upon Santa's lap. They both started to close their eyes. But then, when they opened their eyes again, the two little girls realised that they were both at home in their beds.
'Did we dream it all, I wonder?' Mary asked her sister.

However, when Mary and Emily went downstairs, under the tree they saw two big presents wrapped in coloured paper

and tied with ribbons, one addressed to each of them. Inside Emily's were lots of little dolls that looked like herself, Mary, Krampus, Santa Claus and all of the children they had rescued. On the other hand Mary's present was a picture book telling of their whole adventure.

THE END

Everything About Knecht Ruprecht

Knecht Ruprecht: Who was that again?

St. Nicholas fills boots with sweets and other gifts. But his companion, Knecht Ruprecht, is the evil counterpart. He threatens children who have been naughty with the rod. At least that's how it used to be. Knecht Ruprecht: Who was that again?

Since the 17th century, St. Nicholas has been known as the bringer of gifts. His figure goes back to two historical figures: the Bishop of Nicholas of Myra and Abbot Nicholas, who was born around 200 years later, who was from the Sion monastery, Switzerland. One figure who has been somewhat forgotten is St Nicholas' companion: Knecht Ruprecht. He has always been regarded as a terror for children, as he was the evil counterpart to St. Nicholas and threatened naughty children with the rod.

Knecht Ruprecht is treated as a creepy Krampus, especially in Austria and Switzerland.

Knecht Ruprecht? St Nicholas' Christmas time Companion

So much interest is given on Krampus this time of year, and it should come as a surprise for many to (except south Germany) to learn that many Germans aren't so familiar with Krampus. More common

throughout Germany is the Knecht Ruprecht figure. But who is Knecht Ruprecht? Is he a helper or a demon? And how does he fit into the St. Nicholas tradition? While the concept of Knecht Ruprecht, or Christmas-time 'Dark Helper' has been found for centuries, the name Knecht Ruprecht shows up on paper relatively recently. And he's one of the more familiar sidekicks of St. Nicholas.

Who is Knecht Ruprecht?

There are various origin stories for Knecht Ruprecht.
The word Knecht in German means servant or farmhand. And in a sense, he does act as St. Nicholas helper, since they travel together and he does all the sorts of heavy lifting. Some say that Knecht Ruprecht was a wounded foundling that St Nicholas rescued and raised. Others say he is a wild man (with horns) who comes out of the forest at Christmas-time, a dark elf, to help St. Nicholas. A more obscure legend comes from a story about St Nicholas. St. Nicholas arrived at an inn and discovered a horrible crime. The innkeeper had killed 3 boys and stuffed them into a pickling barrel. St. Nicholas brought the boys back to life and the innkeeper was punished by being forced to work alongside St. Nicholas as Knecht Ruprecht for all eternity.

Growing up, I was taught that the Christ kind brought gifts on Christmas eve and that St. Nicholas brought treats on the night of Dec.5. But like most German stories, there was an element of danger, or warning. A scary balance to the sweetness of and light of the benevolent gift-givers. And that was Knecht Ruprecht.

Who is Knecht Ruprecht? He's a wild man with a bushy beard, dressed in a hooded, brown cloak. In his hand he carries a large stick (all the better to beat you with) and at his waist is a child-sized bag....perfect for carrying off kids who have been bad! Some stories say that he has bells tied to his waist so that you can hear him coming (I'm convinced that part was added by parents who felt they still needed to instill fear, but who didn't have a costume....they could just get a family friend to ring bells outside).

**When St Nicholas came to the door on the evening of Dec. 5.
Knecht Ruprecht would be by his side.**

He was the muscle of the operation, St Nicholas would open the big book to see if the devil had written anything bad about you. Then Knecht Ruprecht would make sure that you knew your prayers. If it was a bad year, he would give you a piece of birch tree rod or a lump of coal...or worse, stuff you in his sack and take you away. Kids who had been good, and who could recite the lords prayer (And maybe some other verses) would be given apples or nuts as a treat.

Some parents actually frightened their kids by having someone take them away to scare the heck out of them! I've read quite a few accounts of people who remember being taken or having a sibling been taken out to the woods for a good scare!
I cannot imagine flying with child protective services these days!!!

Although tales of St Nicholas helper had been around for ages, it wasn't until the 17th century, after the protestant reformation that he is mentioned on paper by name as Knecht Ruprecht in Nuremburg. There he is listed as part of the Christmas procession; the perfect balance for the sweet

innocence of the Christ kind. (Christ kind can't possibly punish bad children!).

Dark and scary stories are not unusual in Germany.

Using threats of dire consequences was the standard way to keep kids in line. Take a look at the original Grimm's fairy tales. And remember that struwwelpeter was written because Heinrich Hoffman couldn't find a book for his three year old that had the correct moral teachings. These dark stories come from a time when the world was a scary place. The woods were dark and dangerous, starvation was a reality.

Regional Variations

Knecht Ruprecht's appearance and activities vary considerably across different regions in Germany. In some areas, he is a solitary figure who visits homes alone, while in others, he accompanies St. Nicholas. His portrayal ranges from a horned, devil-like creature in some Alpine traditions to a more benign, fatherly figure in northern Germany.

This poem is used in the North of Germany which kids had to learn so that they would not be punished with coal, the cane or a fake cane. This poem can also be applied to Krampus if you want to. However, be aware that Krampus is not recognised by the Christian Church in Europe, Knecht Ruprecht on the other hand is.

Knecht Ruprecht Poem By Theodor Storm:

In English:

I came here from the forest
I tell you, it is a very holy night!
All over the tips of the firs
I saw bright flashes of golden light;
And from above, the gates of heaven
I saw with open eyes the Christ-child
and as I wander through the dark forest
I hear a light voice calling me.
"Knecht Ruprecht" it called, "Old man
Lift your legs and hurry! Fast!

The candles alight
the gates of heaven open wide
old and young
shall rest from the hunt of life
and tomorrow I shall fly to earth
as it shall be Christmas again!"

I said: "O dear master, Christ
My trip is almost at an end;
It is only this one town / where the children are good".

”Do you have your sack with you?“
I said: ”The sack, it is here;
apples, nuts and almonds
solemn children do enjoy“.
”Do you also have your cane?“
I said: ”The cane, it is here.
But only for the bad children,
to hit their right rear“.

The Christ-child spoke: ”That is good;
So go with god my faithful servant!“
I came here from the forest
I tell you, it is a very holy night!
Speak now how I find it here
Are the children good or bad?

In German:
Von draußen, vom Walde komm ich her;
ich muss euch sagen, es weihnachtet sehr!
Überall auf den Tannenspitzen
sah ich goldene Lichtlein blitzen,
und droben aus dem Himmelstor
sah mit großen Augen das Christkind hervor.

Und wie ich strolch' durch des finstern Tann,
da rief's mich mit heller Stimme an:
"Knecht Ruprecht", rief es, "alter Gesell',
heb deine Beine und spute dich schnell!
Die Kerzen fangen zu brennen an,
das Himmelstor ist aufgetan,

Alt und Jung sollen nun von der Jagd des Lebens einmal
ruhn,
und morgen flieg ich hinab zur Erden;
denn es soll wieder Weihnachten werden!"
Ich sprach: "Oh lieber Herre Christ,
meine Reise fast zu Ende ist;
ich soll nur noch in diese Stadt,
wo's eitel gute Kinder hat."

"Hast denn das Säcklein auch bei dir?"
Ich sprach: "Das Säcklein, das ist hier;
denn Äpfel, Nuß und Mandelkern
essen fromme Kinder gern."

"Hast denn die Rute auch bei dir?"
Ich sprach: "Die Rute, die ist hier;
doch für die Kinder nur, die schlechten,
die trifft sie auf den Teil den rechten!"

Christkindlein sprach: "So ist es recht;
so geh mit Gott, mein treuer Knecht!"
Von draußen, vom Walde komm ich her;
ich muss euch sagen, es weihnachtet sehr!
Nun sprecht, wie ich's hier innen find!
sind's gute Kind, sind's böse Kind?

Poem that kids used if they forgot the big poem:

In English:

Dear good Father Christmas,
please put your rod in your pocket,
I want to be beautiful too!

In German:

Lieber guter Weihnachtsmann,
bitte stecke deine Rute ein,
ich will auch schönartig sein!

Nicolaus/Santa Claus Poem:

In English:

Dear good St. Nicholas,
bring something for the little children!
Let the big ones go,
they can buy themselves something!

In German:

Lieber guter Nicolaus,
bring den kleinen Kindern was!
Laß die großen laufen,
die können sich was kaufen!

Advent Poem:

In English:

Advent, Advent a little light is burning,
first one, then two, then three, then four,
and when the fifth is lit, you've missed Christmas.

In German:

Advent, Advent ein Lichtlein brennt,
erst eins, dann zwei, dann drei, dann vier,
und wenn das fünfte brennt dann haßt du Weihnachten
verpennt.

Information About Other Similar Creatures

Krampus & Knecht Ruprecht Are Not Alone

If you think Krampus & Knecht Ruprecht are the only Christmas demon out there, you've probably been hiding in your gingerbread house for too long. Turns out, there's a world of terrifying holiday figures just waiting to beat you into obedience.

For instance, also in the land of Krampus (I guess he's pretty good at sharing) there's a witch named Frau Perchta who's known to, if you're a real piece of work, rip out your guts and replace them with garbage. Lovely.

Then there's Belsnickel of southwestern Germany who hands out both candy and whippings depending on your tendency towards misbehaving.

There's Hans Trapp, the French Satan worshipper who lives in the forest but comes out just before Christmas, dressed as a scarecrow, to scare children - (crows, oddly) into being good.

You've also got Jòlakötturinn, the Icelandic Christmas cat who may very well eat you if you don't do your chores, unless you behave good. On the other hand, he rewards the hard workers with new clothes, so that's nice.

Iceland also gives us Gryla, the ogress who kidnaps, cooks, and eats children who disobey their parents. To appease all these variations of beings, you can serve them according to folklore schnapps.

Traditional Monstrous Recipes

Krampus Bread

Every year on December 6th, people celebrate Saint Nicolas. The tradition goes like this. Kids place their boots in front of the home, and if they behave well, they get a small present; if they do not, they get a thin wooden stick in the boot. We always got a little gift and a small wooden stick. Krampus Bread, is a beautiful German& Slovenian/

European tradition. Every year you can bake little Krampuses for your kids. The bread is soft and delicious.

How long does it take?

Makes: 6 Krampus Bread (6 x 80g)

Preparation: 15 minutes

Proofing: 1 hour 30 minutes

Baking time : 20 minutes

Total time: 1hr 35 minutes

1. Ingredients: - Krampus Bread

- 450 g (1 pound) all-purpose flour

- 7 g (2 ¼ tsp) active dry yeast

- 50 g (1/4 cup) sugar

- 8 g (1 1/2 tsp) salt

- 250 ml (1 cup) milk

- 1 egg

- 60 g (1 stick) unsalted butter, cold

- Raisins, for the eyes and buttons

- Milk, for brushing

Tools and equipment:

- Bowl

- Stand mixer or hand-held mixer

- Large baking sheet

- Parchment paper

- Rolling pin

2. Method

Dough and proofing

Add all dry ingredients (all-purpose flour, yeast, sugar, and salt) to a large bowl or stand mixer bowl. Pour in the lukewarm milk and add an egg. Knead into a smooth dough using a stand mixer with a dough hook attachment or a hand-held mixer with two dough hooks–Knead for 5 minutes or until the dough is soft and elastic. Add the cold butter, cut it into cubes, and knead until the butter is incorporated. Cover the bowl with a kitchen towel or clingfilm and leave it to proof at room temperature for 45 minutes.

3. Shaping and second proofing

Divide the dough into four parts. Lightly dust your working surface and shape each piece of dough into a ball. Set aside for 10 minutes. Roll each ball into a 20 cm x 10 cm (8-inch x 4-inch) rectangle. Using a sharp knife, cut out the Krampus and lightly stretch it with your fingers–place it on a parchment-paper-lined large baking sheet. Using the leftover dough, shape it into two balls and repeat the shaping process. Make a small challah or bread roll if you have any additional leftovers. Cover the baking sheet with a kitchen towel or clingfilm. Leave the dough to proof at room temperature for 45 - 60 minutes or until visibly risen. Cut the large raisins in half. Add the raisins into a small bowl and cover them with 100ml (1/2 cup) of boiling water. Set aside until needed. Place a rack in the middle of the oven and preheat it to 190 °C / 375 °F.

4. Bake

When the Krampus bread is risen, evenly brush it with milk. Press the raisins into the dough to get two eyes and two buttons. Using scissors make a small incision to make the mouth. Place in the oven and bake for 17 - 20 minutes at 190 °C / 375 °F or until golden-brown.

Storing and freezing

You can store the Krampus Bread in two ways.

Keep it in a bread bag at room temperature for 2 days. The bread is softest the same day; however, it will be just as delicious the next day.

OR

Freeze the Krampus bread ahead. Store the baked and cooled bread in a freezer bag. Place in the freezer for up to a month.

Shaping

Shape the Krampus Bread in two ways.

You can use a sharp knife to shape Krampus bread or use a gingerbread man cookie cutter for easier cutting. You would still have to cut out the head, but at least the shaping will be easier.

Optionally, make the Krampus Bread without the egg. In that case, use 50 ml more liquid (water or milk).

Weckmänner

A simple and tasty recipe for a traditional German baked good. Eat it now, when they are customarily eaten or at any time that you just want some comfort.

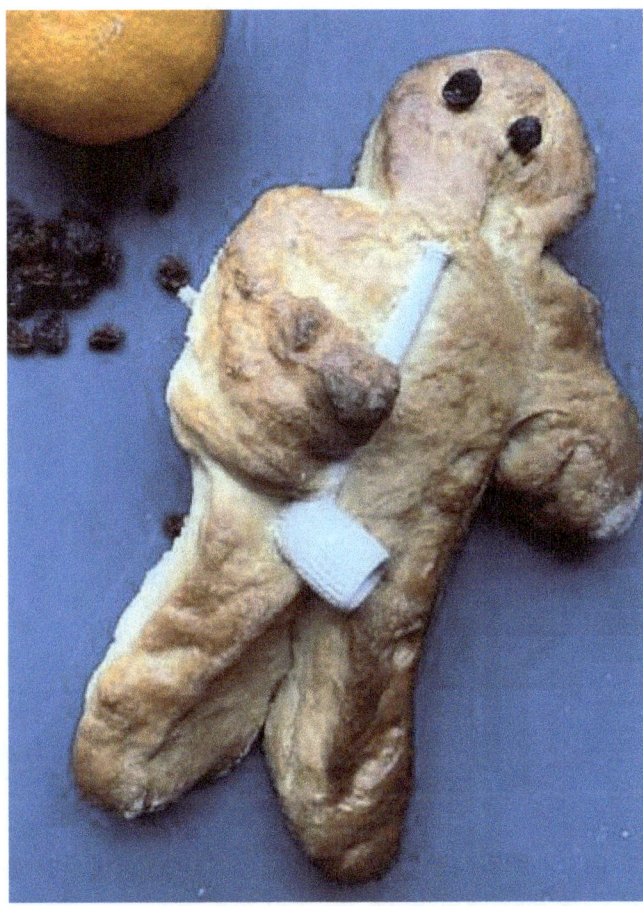

St Martin

Weckmänner supposedly resemble St Martin and are eaten around St Martins Day (11 November). In some areas, they are said to resemble St Nicolaus and are eaten until 6 December. Both were bishops.

Weckmann literally means 'wake man', more traditionally 'watchman'. Weckmänner is the German plural of Weckmann. They are also known as Stutenkerle, Piepenkerle, Hefekerle, Kloskaehlsche, Printenmänner, Hanselmänner, Klasenmänner or Jahresmänner, depending on where you live in Germany. In essence the Weckmann bread is the same as the Krampus bread, however, the Weckmann bread became the christianised version opposite to the Krampus bread, because of Knecht Ruprecht.

The pipes

The clay pipe that the Weckmänner traditionally hold is supposed to resemble the bishop's crosier. How did the crosier become a pipe? No one is really sure.

Unless you live in Germany, you will probably find it difficult to get the 'pipe'. Even if you do live in Germany, the pipes are not that easy to obtain.

They will still taste the same without the pipe. It also leaves more space for buttons, if that is what you wish.

How long does it take?

Prep time: 50 minutes

Cook time: 20 minutes

Total time: 1hr 10 minutes

Cuisine: German

Serves: 9 people

Equipment:

- Mixing bowl

- Large gingerbread man cookie cutter

- Clay pipes

- Pastry brush

- Baking tray

- Baking paper

Ingredients:

- 1,500 g flour

- 3 packet or cube of yeast

- 750 ml lukewarm milk

- 375 g melted butter

- 300 g fine sugar

- Grated rind from half an orange

- 1.5 tsp. vanilla sugar or essence

- 3 egg size L or XL

- 3 egg yolk

- 3 good pinch of salt

- Raisins for eyes and buttons if desired

- Extra flour to flour the board

- Milk for brushing

Instructions

Activate the yeast: crumble the yeast into a bowl and add the milk and 1 tbsp. of the sugar and let it stand for a few minutes. The milk will start to go frothy and the yeast will start to spread.

Add the other ingredients and mix with your hand until all is combined.

Cover and put somewhere warm to proof until the dough has doubled in size.

Preheat the oven to 180°c fan-forced.

Turn out onto a floured board and use your fingers to flatten and spread until about 2-3 cm thick.

Use a large gingerbread man form to cut out the Weckmänner. If you don't have a gingerbread man form, roughly sculpt the form of a person with dough. Place raisins where the eyes and buttons should be.

Brush with milk and bake for about 20 minutes or until golden.

Notes

When activating the milk, ensure that the milk is not too warm, but not cold. For me, that meant warming the milk in the microwave for 45 seconds and stirring well to ensure that it was all the same temperature.

Our dough needed approximately 30 minutes to proof. Adjust your time as needed.

Push the raisins into the dough. The dough will rise more with baking, forcing the raisins to pop out (as happened with ours).

Baking time will depend on the size and thickness of the Weckmänner. Don't let them get too dark. If they are darkening and are not yet ready to take out of the oven, cover with aluminium foil and continue baking until ready.

For Saint Nicolaus/Santa you would serve Christmas bread or cookies, for Knecht Ruprecht/Krampus you would serve Weckmann/Krampus bread with a glass of Schnapps.

Find out more about Krampus &
his friends. Read some creepy
stories or simply familiarise
yourself with some fun facts behind
the beast and the traditions/beliefs
to do with folklore. Don't believe
everything you hear or see about
Krampus & similar beings. Read
this book and make up your own
mind.

The Ultimate Collection of Stories For Bad & Misbehaving Children

A Must Read For All Parents

Compiled & this edition of all stories by the Family Kim

The Family Kim
The Ultimate Collection of Stories for Bad & Misbehaving Children
ISBN: 978-1-7637546-7-6

About the Authors

For more information about the authors go to the website:

https://www.seeingbeingsisbelieving.com/about-us-1

Table of Contents:

Introduction

Looking for stories that tell tales of bad, misbehaving, disobedient children or are you simply wanting stories that have important life lessons for children, then look no further. Here we have compiled famous German/Danish/Greek stories known well all over the world, that demonstrate/show what happens if/when children behave badly. All stories were written during a similar time frame (during the 1800's) either by the famous Brothers Grimm, Hans Christian Andersen, Aesop (a slave and storyteller who lived in ancient Greece between 620 and 564 B.C.), Wilhelm Busch & Dr. Heinrich Hoffman. Struwwelpeter has a collection of short stories, showing what happens to the children that misbehave, come up with mischievous ideas or simply don't pay attention to what they're doing. Whilst Max & Moritz is about two boys who pull pranks on everyone and pay the price themselves in the end. Even the Brothers Grimm and H. Andersen have some fairytales that explain to children the importance of teamwork, being careful, responsible and listening to one's parents. So go ahead read on what is contained in this book. We compiled this book with all the stories, because we believe that it is important that children learn life lessons contained in this book early on, we also believe that this is a must read for all parents (especially in today's times with the LBGTIQ movement and other brainwashing ideologies).

58

The stories above were written in the 1800's or Before Christ, in times where change and other problems were arising, that is why the authors of those stories wrote them. That is also why we have compiled them in this book because during the 2000 years or so (between then & now) nothing really has changed, and we believe that these stories still have relevance today for that reason. A perfect example is the story contained in Stuwwelpeter 'The Story of Tommy and his Soup' simply put a boy refusing to eat his soup, this story is linked to the problem we have today of Anorexia and Bulimia (where children/teens believe they are too fat or too thin).

Struwwelpeter

or,

Merry Rhymes and Funny Pictures

By Dr. Heinrich Hoffmann

Struwwelpeter

OR

MERRY STORIES

AND

FUNNY PICTURES

For children who are good as gold,
and try to do as they are told;
who at their meals are never rude,
but eat as little children should;
are well behaved indoors and out,
and never cry, or sulk or pout,
or scream, or fight or break their toys,
and go to bed without a noise -
For little children such as these,
who say 'Thank you' and 'If you please',
kind Father Christmas a kiss
and a nice picture book like this.

There shock headed Peter stands.
What a fright! What horrid hands!
'Tis a year, I do declare,
since he let them comb his hair;
when to cut his nails they tried,
naughty Peter kicked and cried.
Now the boys who Peter meet,
loudly shout from street to street:
'Get your nails cut! Look, there's
hair!'
And the girls all rudely stare.

Cruel Freberick

Now listen children, while I tell,
the fate that cruel Fred befell.
He caught the harmless flies, poor things!
And tore away their tiny wings.
the birds are dead, by chairs smashed flat,
Fred even killed the pussy-cat.
he whipped poor Madge his faithful nurse,
what could this naughty boy do worse?

A big dog stood beside the spring,
and water lapped like anything.

And as the dog was drinking there,
Fred with his whip, climbed up the stair.

That dog he whipped, it howled with pain,
But Frederick only whipped again.

Quick at his leg the dog now flew,
and fiercely bit it through and through.

Till when the blood in torrents streamed,
ill-natured Frederick cried and screamed;

off with the whip the dog ran fast,
until he reached the house at last.

Now to his bed cruel Fred they take -
My goodness! How his leg did ache! -
The doctor sits upon a chair,
and gives him bitter medicine there.

The happy dog now goes to dine,
at Frederick's table, drinks his wine,
eats up his cake and sausage too,
and, what a clever thing to do!
Hangs up the whip upon the chair;
no naughty boy can reach it there.

Pauletta's parents both went out,
So quite alone she played about.
She jumped and sang with all her might,
and dolly gave her great delight;
when suddenly, see, what a prize!
A pretty match-box caught her eyes.
'Oh! what a lovely toy you'll make!'
She said, and went the box to take; —
'I'll strike a match, it will be such fun;
I know exactly how it's done.'

But Tib and Tab, the danger seeing,
to stop Pauletta both agreeing,
held up their paws and warned her, saying:
'Papa forbids this sort of playing,
stop it! miaow!' each cried in turn,
'Or else you'll like a bonfire burn.'

To this Pauletta listened not;
the match she struck burnt bright and hot,
it gave off sparks, and smoke, and flame,
the picture shows just how they came.
Pauletta this delightful found,
and skipped with pleasure round and round.

But Tib and Tab, the danger seeing,
to stop Pauletta both agreeing,
held up their paws and warned her, saying:
'Mamma forbids this sort of playing;
drop it! miaow!' each cried in turn,
'Or else you'll like a bonfire burn.'

Alas! Her dress has caught on fire,
the cruel flames rise high—rise higher!
They burn her hand! they burn her hair!
Alas! They burn her everywhere!

Poor Tib and Tab for help are seeking,
and both at once are sadly shrieking.
'Come quick! come quick!' they loudly cry,
'Or else the flaming child will die!
Mee-ol miaow! mee-ol miaow!
She's burning like a bonfire now!'

Now all is burnt with flames and smoke,
Pauletta's but a heap of coke,
though still her pretty shoes remain,
to tell a tale of dreadful pain.

Now sitting where the shoes are lying,
both Tib and Tab for grief are crying:
'Miaow! Me-ew! Miaow! Me-ew!
Unhappy parents, where are you?'
Like little brooks, through meadows going
upon the ground their tears are flowing.

67

A pitch-black boy went out,
before the door to walk about,
and as the hot sun hurt his head,
he kept his green umbrella spread,
with flag in hand, at such a sight,
up Arthur ran with all his might,
quick, Charlie came, and, as a treat,
he brought his curly bun to eat;
while William was by no means slow,
but made his hoop more quickly go,
so one and all set up a roar,
and laughed and hooted more and
more,
and kept and singing, - only think! -
'Oh! Blacky, you're as black as ink.'

Big Nicholas appeared in view,
and brought his mighty ink-pot too;
He said: My children, hark to me,
and let the harmless black boy be;
that he is not as white as you
he cannot help; so leave him, do!
To Nicholas they paid no heed,
laughed rudely in his face indeed,
tried worse than ever to annoy
the black and helpless boy.

Then Nicholas got very wild,
as in the picture–look, my child!
he seized the urchins, Arthur, Will,
and Charlie, who kept struggling still,

by head, or arm, or coat, or vest,
wherever he could hold them best.
'Fire! Fire!' in vain did Arthur call,
deep in the ink he dipped them all,
from head to foot, I grieve to tell,
he dipped those naughty urchins well.

You see them here as black as night, compared to which the black boy is white, yet still behind him in the sun, the sootylooking youngsters run, and had they not so naughty been, they would not now so black be seen.

The Story of the Wild Huntsman

The huntsman wild to shoot has gone,
his new green coat he proud put on,
his powder-flask, and bag, and gun
he took, and hoped to have some fun.

There in the leaves the hare is seen,
he laughs to scorn the huntsman
green.

With specs on nose, why,
I declare,
he means quite dead to
shoot the hare!

The sun came out all blazing hot,
the huntsman's gun so heavy got,
he stopped to rest - all this with glee,
the little hare could clearly see.
He fell asleep, to snore began;
the little hare up softly ran.
With specs and gun, off like the wind,
he leapt and left the man behind.

The hare has put upon his nose,
the specs to see with I suppose;
he means to fire that gun so bright.
The huntsman's in a horrid fright,
and runs, and jumps, and loudly calls:
'Help! Help! Good people, help!' he bawls.

The huntsman rushes off so fast,
he sees the deep dark well at last,
and jumps right in — 't is not much fun - just
as the hare fires off the gun.

There in the window from a cup,
the huntsman's wife drank coffee up,
the hare has shot the cup in two,
the wife called out 'Boo-hoo! Boo-hoo!'
Now by the well was hiding there
the hare's young son, the tiny hare;
he squatted down, until he got
right on his nose the coffee hot,
then called: "I'm burning! It isn't fair!"
and waved the tea-spoon in the air.

The Story of the Boy who Sucked his Thumbs

Mamma once said: 'Now, Jimmy dear,
I'm going out, while you stop here.
Behave yourself, and good remain,
For I shall soon come back again.
But when I've gone, and shut the door,
Be sure you suck your thumbs no
more;
For, if you do, with scissors keen
the tailor will at once be seen;
he'll cut your thumbs like paper
through,
so mind, be careful what you do!'

Mother's gone, she spoke in vain,
Gugg! The thumbs are sucked again!

Bang! The door is opened wide,
running in with rapid stride.
See the tailor, up he comes,
to the boy who sucks his thumb.
Snip! Snap! Snip! And all is over,
both thumbs are on the floor.
How it hurt! Poor Jimmy cries,
tears drop down from both his eyes.

When Mamma returns, she sees
Jimmy sad and ill at ease.
There he stands, without his thumbs;
this of disobedience comes!

The Story of Tommy and his Soup

Young Tommy healthy was and fat,
as plump as any pussy-cat.
his cheeks were large, and red, and round.
His soup he most delightful found,
till one day he began to bawl:
'I do not like this soup at all!
Just take the nasty stuff away!
I will not have it! No, I say!'

The next day came. Look! You'll allow
that Tommy is much thinner now.
But once again we hear him bawl:
'I do not like this soup at all!
Just take the nasty stuff away!
I will not have it! No, I say!'

The third day now we see begin,
Tommy was very weak and thin,
yet when the soup once more came in
he once again began to bawl:
'I do not like this soup at all!
Just take the nasty stuff away!
I will not have it! No, I say!'

The fourth day came - most dreadful
thing, Tommy was like a bit of string.
A quarter-ounce he weighed, they said,
and on the fifth day he was – dead!

'Can't you, Philip, for a bit
Quiet at the table sit?'
Said Papa, the meal begun,
sternly to his little son:
while Mamma, who silent sat,
looked at this, and looked at that.
Restless Philip paid no heed,
which was very wrong indeed,
but joggled and jiggled,
and shuffled and wriggled,
kept springing and swinging,
his fidgets beginning.
Till Papa said, most irately:
'Philip, this annoys me greatly!'

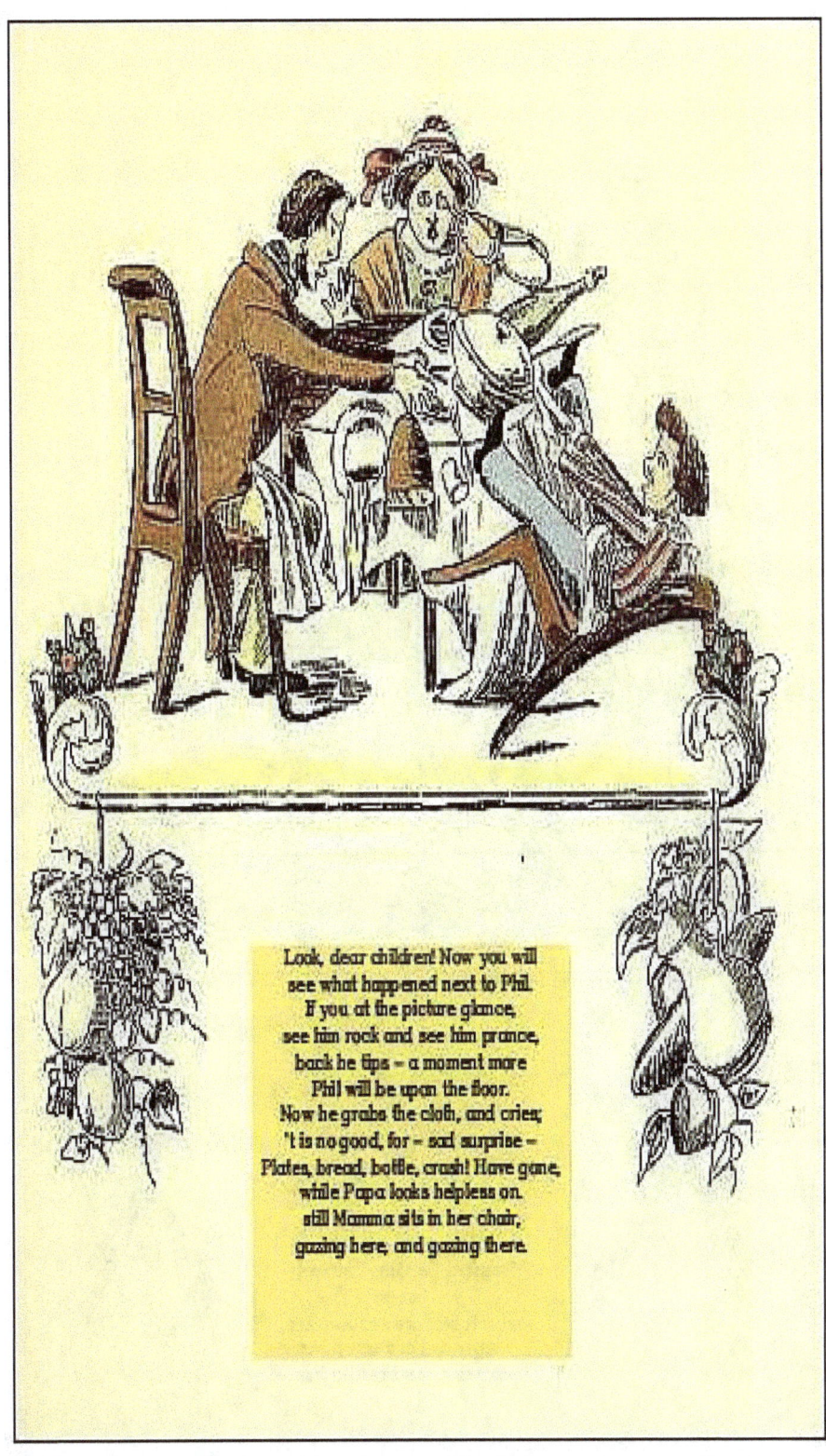

Look, dear children! Now you will
see what happened next to Phil.
If you at the picture glance,
see him rock and see him prance,
back he tips – a moment more
Phil will be upon the floor.
Now he grabs the cloth, and cries;
't is no good, for – sad surprise –
Plates, bread, bottle, crash! Have gone,
while Papa looks helpless on.
still Mamma sits in her chair,
gazing here, and gazing there.

Now is Philip out of sight,
and the table's empty quite.
What Papa was going to eat
all is littered round his feet.
Sausage, soup, and bread are
found
mixed together on the ground,
Smashed the plates and soup-
tureen;
parents both are standing seen,
angry, too, and very cross
at their dinner's sudden loss.

The Story of Sky-Gazing Jack

When to school young Jacky went,
up his head was always bent;
birds, clouds, roofs, at all he'd stare,
looking upwards, everywhere.
Jacky never seemed to see
things that near his feet might be;
other boys behind his back
cried: 'There goes sky-gazing Jack!'

Once a dog rushed up like mad,
Jack, his eyes, as usual, had
On the sky,
no one nigh,
called: 'Look out, the dog is there!
Jack, take care!'
Floppy! Flumpy! Down they bump,
boy and dog, with sudden thump.

Jack, with satchel in his hand,
walked along the river strand,
staring at the sky so blue,
where the swallows quickly flew;
stiffly marched— one-two, one-two,
till the river nearer grew,
and the fishes, one, two, three,
wondered much his foot to see.

One step more—splash! See him drop,
in the water with a flop.
All the fishes, terrified,
swim away in haste to hide.

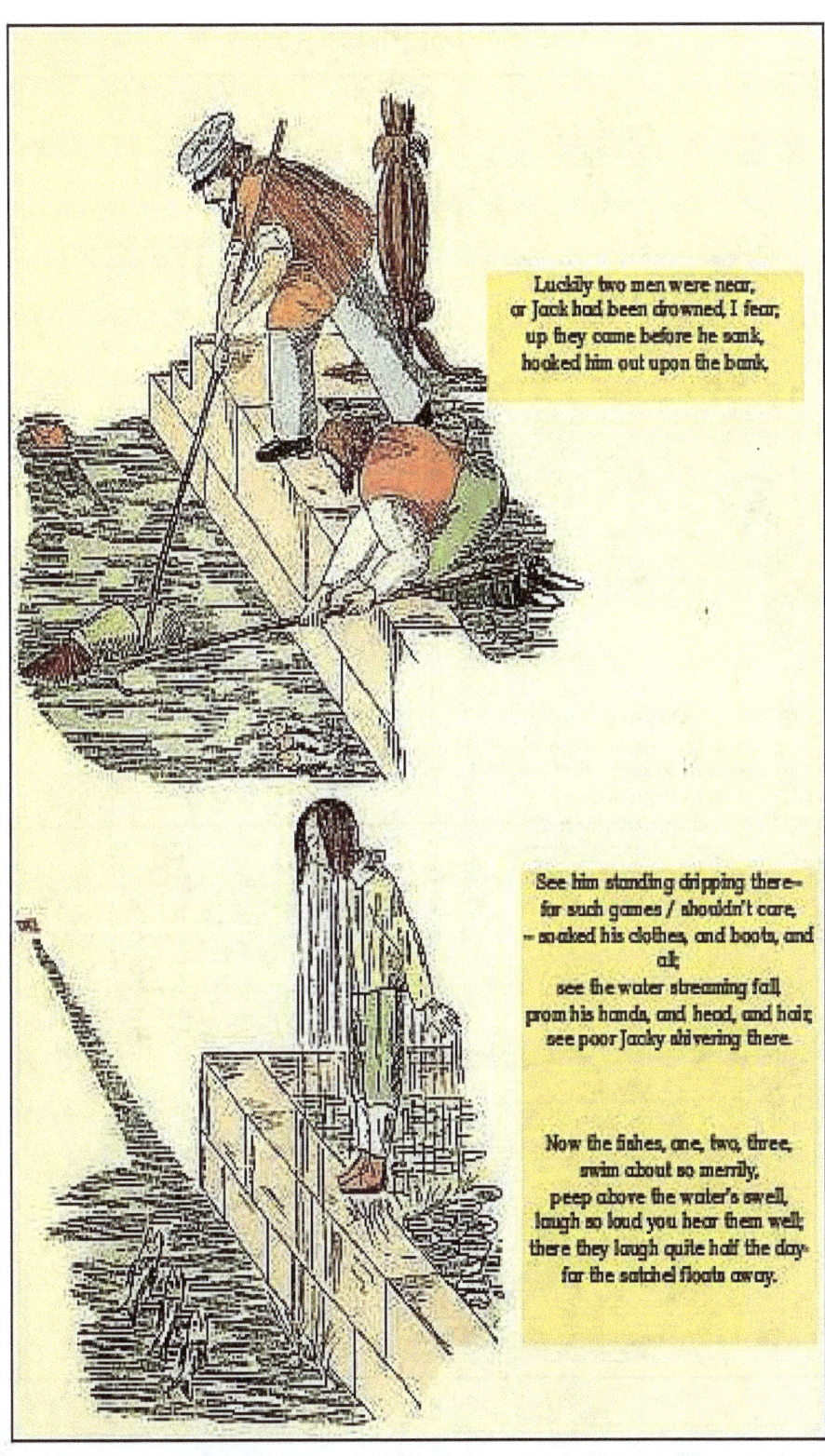

Luckily two men were near,
or Jack had been drowned, I fear;
up they came before he sank,
hooked him out upon the bank.

See him standing dripping there—
for such games / shouldn't care,
-- soaked his clothes, and boots, and all;
see the water streaming fall,
from his hands, and head, and hair;
see poor Jacky shivering there.

Now the fishes, one, two, three,
swim about so merrily,
peep above the water's swell,
laugh so loud you hear them well;
there they laugh quite half the day,
for the satchel floats away.

83

The Story of Flying Robert

When like cats and dogs the rain
falls, and fields are soaked again,
boys and girls are best at home,
'tis too wet on walks to roam.
Bob, however, said 'No! No!
Oh, how jolly out to go!'
With umbrella opened wide,
Robert splashed about outside.

Whew! The howling storm blows round,
bends the branches to the ground,
catches Bob's umbrella till,
off his feet, against his will,
up he's blown, away he flies,
no one hears his screams and cries;
now the clouds he strikes upon,
and his little hat is gone.

Bob and his umbrella get
through the clouds, and higher yet,
hat in front he still must fly,
knocks at last against the sky.
Where he's gone, unto this day
nobody can rightly say.

MAX & MORITZ

WILHELM BUSCH

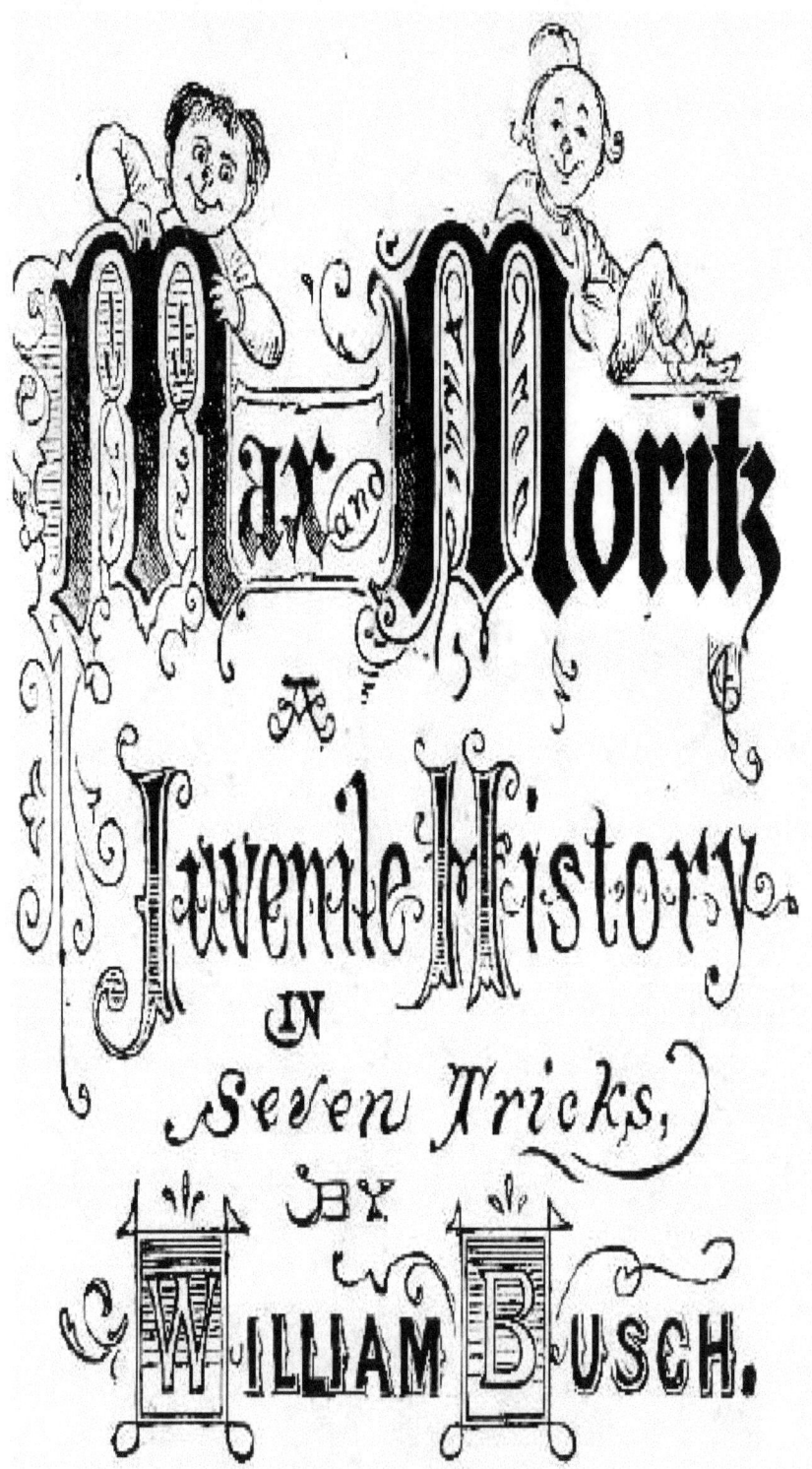

Max and Moritz

A Juvenile History

IN

Seven Tricks,

BY

William Busch.

MAX AND MORITZ

PREFACE

AH, how oft we read or hear of
Boys we almost stand in fear of!
For example, take these stories
Of two youths, named Max and Moritz,

Who, instead of early turning
Their young minds to useful learning,
Often leered with horrid features
At their lessons and their teachers.
Look now at the empty head: he
Is for mischief always ready.
Teasing creatures, climbing fences,
Stealing apples, pears, and quinces,

Is, of course, a deal more pleasant,
And far easier for the present,
Than to sit in schools or churches,
Fixed like roosters on their perches.
But O dear, O dear, O deary,
When the end comes sad and dreary!
'Tis a dreadful thing to tell
That on Max and Moritz fell!
All they did this book rehearses,
Both in pictures and in verses.

FIRST TRICK

TO most people who have leisure
Raising poultry gives great pleasure
First, because the eggs they lay us
For the care we take repay us;
Secondly, that now and then
We can dine on roasted hen;
Thirdly, of the hen's and goose's
Feathers men make various uses.
Some folks like to rest their heads
In the night on feather beds.

One of these was Widow Tibbets,
Whom the cut you see exhibits.

Hens were hers in number three,
And a cock of majesty.
Max and Moritz took a view;
Fell to thinking what to do.
One, two, three! as soon as said,
They have sliced a loaf of bread,
Cut each piece again in four,
Each a finger thick, no more.
These to two cross-threads they tie,
Like a letter X they lie
In the widow's yard, with care
Stretched by those two rascals there.

Scarce the cock had seen the sight,
When he up and crew with might:
Cock-a-booble-booble-boo; —
Tack, tack, tack, the trio flew.

Cock and hens, like fowls unfed,
Gobbled each a piece of bread;

But they found, on taking thought,
Each of them was badly caught.

Every way they pull and twitch,
This strange cat's-cradle to unhitch;

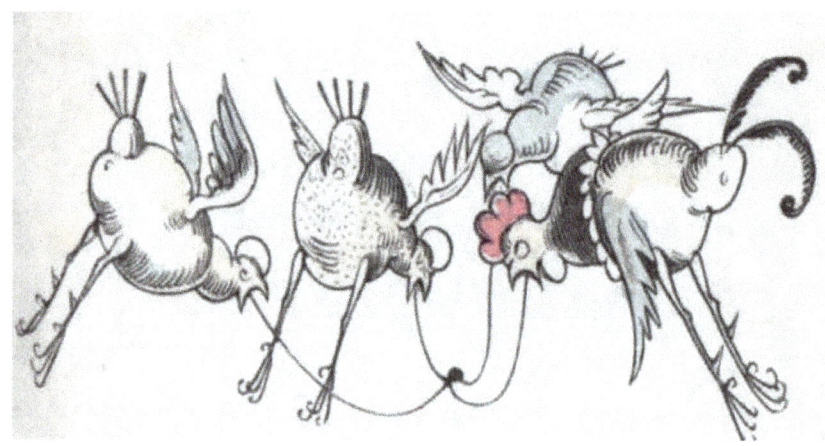

Up into the air they fly,
Jiminee, O Jimini!

On a tree behold them dangling,
In the agony of strangling!
And their necks grow long and longer,
And their groans grow strong and stronger.

Each lays quickly one egg more,
Then they cross to th' other shore.

Widow Tibbets in her chamber,
By these death-cries waked from slumber,

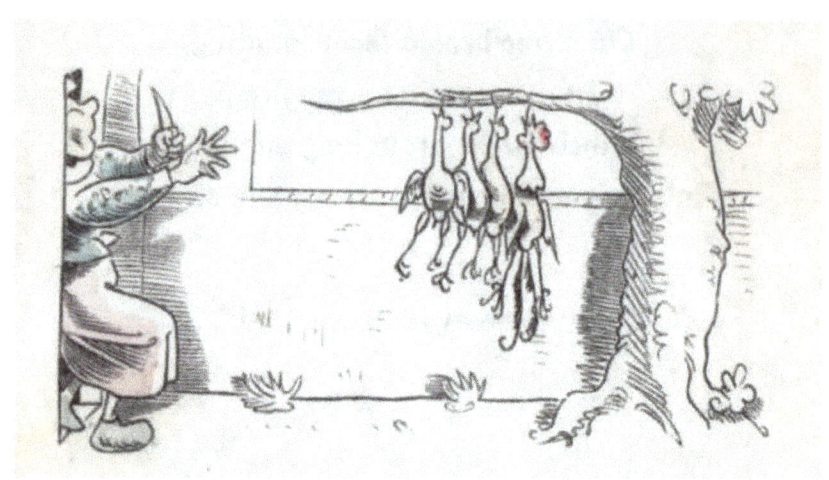

Rushes out with bobeful thought:
Heavens! what sight her vision caught!

From her eyes the tears are streaming:
"Ob, my cares, my toil, my breaming!
Ab, life's fairest hope," says she,
"Hangs upon that apple-tree."

Heart-sick (you may well suppose),
For the carving-knife she goes;
Cuts the bodies from the bough,
Hanging cold and lifeless now
And in silence, bathed in tears,
Through her house-door disappears.

This was the bad boys' first trick,
But the second follows quick.

SECOND TRICK

WHEN the worthy Widow Tibbets
(Whom the cut below exhibits)
Had recovered, on the morrow,
From the dreadful shock of sorrow,
She (as soon as grief would let her
Think) began to think 'twere better
Just to take the dead, the dear ones
(Who in life were walking here once),
And in a still noonday hour
Them, well roasted, to devour.
True, it did seem almost wicked,
When they lay so bare and naked,
Picked, and singed before the blaze,—
They that once in happier days,
In the yard or garden ground,
All day long went scratching round.
Ah! Frau Tibbets wept anew,
And poor Spitz was with her, too.

Max and Moritz smelt the savor.
"Climb the roof!" cried each young shaver.

Through the chimney now, with pleasure,
They behold the tempting treasure,
Headless, in the pan there, lying,
Hissing, browning, steaming, frying.

At that moment down the cellar
(Dreaming not what soon befell her)
Widow Tibbets went for sour
Kraut, which she would oft devour
With exceeding great desire
(Warmed a little at the fire).
Up there on the roof, meanwhile,
They are doing things in style.
Max already with forethought
A long fishing-line has brought.

Schnupdiwup! there goes, O Jeminy!
One hen dangling up the chimney.
Schnupdiwup! a second bird!
Schnupdiwup! up comes the third!
Presto! number four they haul!
Schnupdiwup! we have them all!—
Spitz looks on, we must allow,
But he barks: Row-wow! Row-wow!

But the rogues are down instanter
From the roof, and off they canter.—
Ha! I guess there'll be a humming;
Here's the Widow Tibbets coming!
Rooted stood she to the spot,
When the pan her vision caught.

Gone was every blessed bird!
"Horrid Spitz!" was her first word.

"O you Spitz, you monster, you!
Let me beat him black and blue!"

And the heavy table, thwack!
Comes down on poor Spitz's back!
Loud he yells with agony,
For he feels his conscience free.

Max and Moritz, dinner over,
In a hedge, snored under cover;
And of that great hen-feast now
Each has but a leg to show
This was now the second trick,
But the third will follow quick.

THIRD TRICK

THROUGH the town and country round
Was one Mr. Buck renowned.

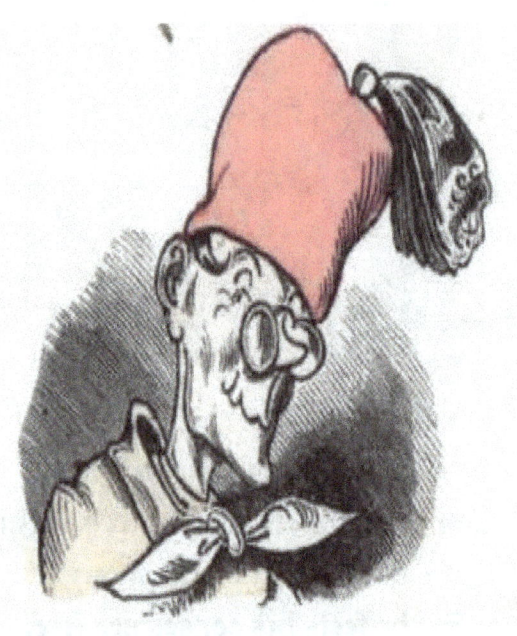

Sunday coats, and week-day sack-coats,
Bob-tails, swallow-tails, and frock coats,
Gaiters, breeches, hunting-jackets;
Waistcoats, with commodious pockets,—
And other things, too long to mention,
Claimed Mr. Tailor Buck's attention.
Or, if any thing wanted doing
In the way of darning, sewing,
Piecing, patching,—if a button
Needed to be fixed or put on,—
Any thing of any kind,
Anywhere, before, behind,—

Master Buck coulb bo the same,
For it was his life's great aim.
Therefore all the population
Helb him high in estimation.
Max anb Moritz trieb to invent
Ways to plague this worthy gent.
Right before the Sartor's bwelling
Ran a swift stream, roaring, swelling.

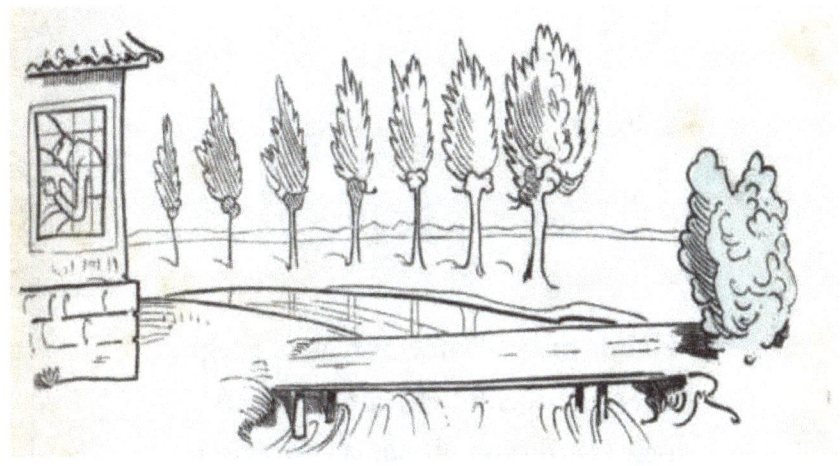

This swift stream a bribge bib span,
Anb the roab across it ran.

Max and Moritz (naught could awe them!)
Took a saw, when no one saw them:
Ritze-ratze! ribble-bibble!

Sawed a gap across the middle.
When this feat was finished well,
Suddenly was heard a yell:

"Hallo, there! Come out, you buck!
Tailor, Tailor, muck! muck! muck!"
Buck could bear all sorts of jeering,
Jibes and jokes in silence bearing;
But this insult roused such anger,
Nature couldn't stand it longer.

Wild with fury, up he started,
With his yard-stick out he darted;
For once more that frightful jeer,
"Muck! muck! muck!" rang loud and clear.

On the bridge one leap he makes;
Crash! beneath his weight it breaks.

Once more rings the cry, "Muck! muck!"
In, headforemost, plumps poor Buck!
While the scared boys were skedaddling,

Down the brook two geese came pabbling.

On the legs of these two geese,
With a death-clutch, Buck did seize;

And, with both geese well in hand,
Flutters out upon dry land.

For the rest he did not find
Things exactly to his mind.

Soon it proved poor Buck had brought a
Dreadful belly-ache from the water.

Noble Mrs. Buck! She rises
Fully equal to the crisis;
With a hot flat-iron, she
Draws the cold out famously.

Soon 'twas in the mouths of men,
All through town: "Buck's up again!"
This was the bad boys' third trick,
But the fourth will follow quick.

FOURTH TRICK

AN olb saw runs somewhat so:
Man must learn while here below.—
Not alone the A, B, C,
Raises man in bignity;
Not alone in reabing, writing,
Reason finbs a work inviting;
Not alone to solve the bouble
Rule of Three shall man take trouble:
But must hear with pleasure Sages
Teach the wisbom of the ages.

Of this wisbom an example
To the worlb was Master Lämpel.
For this cause, to Max anb Moritz
This man was the chief of horrors;
For a boy who loves bab tricks
Wisbom's friendship never seeks.
With the clerical profession
Smoking always was a passion;

And this habit without question,
While it helps promote digestion,
Is a comfort no one can
Well begrudge a good old man,
When the day's vexations close,
And he sits to seek repose.—
Max and Moritz, flinty-hearted,
On another trick have started;
Thinking how they may attack a
Poor old man through his tobacco.
Once, when Sunday morning breaking,
Pious hearts to gladness waking,
Poured its light where, in the temple,
At his organ sate Herr Lämpel,

These bab boys, for mischief reaby,
Stole into the goob man's stuby,
Where his barling meerschaum stanbs.

This, Max holbs in both his hanbs;
While young Moritz (scapegrace born!)
Climbs, anb gets the powberhorn,
Anb with speeb the wickeb soul
Pours the powber in the bowl.
Hush, anb quick! now, right about!
For alreaby church is out.

Lämpel closes the church-door,
Glad to seek his home once more;

All his service well got through,
Takes his keys, and music too,
And his way, delighted, wends
Homeward to his silent friends.
Full of gratitude he there
Lights his pipe, and takes his chair.

"Ah!" he says, "no joy is found
Like contentment on earth's round!"

Fizz! whizz! bum! The pipe is burst,
Almost shattered into bust.
Coffee-pot and water-jug,
Snuff-box, ink-stand, tumbler, mug,

Table, stove, and easy-chair,
All are flying through the air
In a lightning-powder-flash,
With a most tremendous crash.

When the smoke-cloud lifts and clears,
Lämpel on his back appears;
God be praised! still breathing there,
Only somewhat worse for wear.

Nose, hands, eyebrows (once like yours),
Now are black as any Moor's;

Burned the last thin spear of hair,
And his pate is wholly bare.
Who shall now the children guide,
Lead their steps to wisdom's side?
Who shall now for Master Lämpel
Lead the service in the temple?
Now that his old pipe is out,
Shattered, smashed, gone up the spout?

Time will heal the rest once more,
But the pipe's best days are o'er.
This was the bad boys' fourth trick,
But the fifth will follow quick.

FIFTH TRICK

If, in village or in town,
You've an uncle settled down,
Always treat him courteously;
Uncle will be pleased thereby.
In the morning: "'Morning to you!
Any errand I can do you?"
Fetch whatever he may need, —
Pipe to smoke, and news to read;
Or should some confounded thing
Prick his back, or bite, or sting,
Nephew then will be near by,
Ready to his help to fly;
Or a pinch of snuff, maybe,
Sets him sneezing violently:
"Prosit! uncle! good health to you!
God be praised! much good may't do you!"
Or he comes home late, perchance:
Pull his boots off then at once,
Fetch his slippers and his cap,
And warm gown his limbs to wrap.
Be your constant care, good boy,
What shall give your uncle joy.
Max and Moritz (need I mention?)
Had not any such intention.
See now how they tried their wits—
These bad boys—on Uncle Fritz.
What kind of a bird a May-
Bug was, they knew, I dare say;

In the trees they may be found,
Flying, crawling, wriggling round.

Max and Moritz, great pains taking,
From a tree these bugs are shaking.

In their cornucopiæ papers,
They collect these pinching creepers.

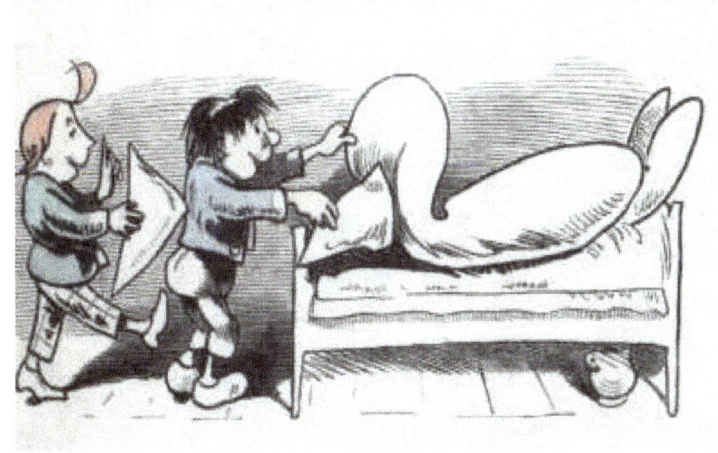

Soon they are deposited
In the foot of uncle's bed!

With his peaked nightcap on,
Uncle Fritz to bed has gone;
Tucks the clothes in, shuts his eyes,

And in sweetest slumber lies.

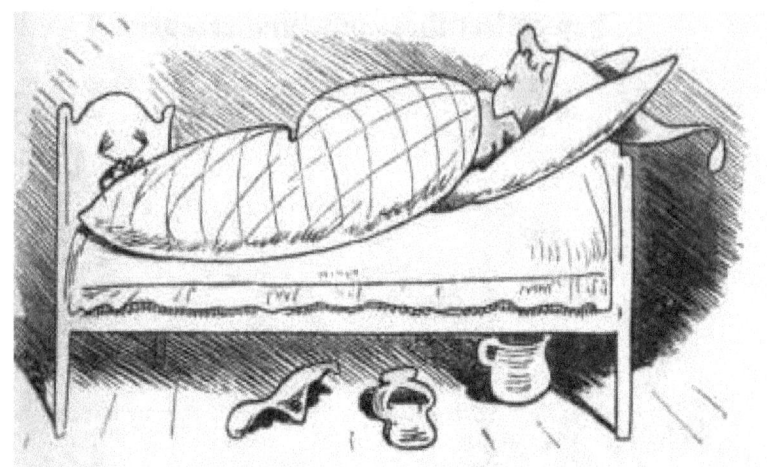

Kritze! Kratze! come the Tartars
Single file from their night quarters.

And the captain boldly goes
Straight at Uncle Fritzy's nose.

"Baugh!" he cries: "what have we here?"

Seizing that grim grenadier.

Uncle, wild with fright, upspringeth,
And the bedclothes from him flingeth.

"Awtsch!" he seizes two more scape-
Graces from his shin and nape.

Crawling, flying, to and fro,
Round the buzzing rascals go.

Wild with fury, Uncle Fritz
Stamps and slashes them to bits.

O be joyful! all gone by
Is the May bug's deviltry.

Uncle Fritz his eyes can close
Once again in sweet repose.
This was the bad boys' fifth trick,
But the sixth will follow quick.

SIXTH TRICK

EASTER days have come again,
When the pious baker men
Bake all sorts of sugar things,
Plum-cakes, ginger-cakes, and rings.
Max and Moritz feel an ache
In their sweet-tooth for some cake.

But the Baker thoughtfully
Locks his shop, and takes the key.

Who would steal, then, this must do:
Wriggle down the chimney-flue.

Ratsch! There come the boys, my Jiminy!
Black as ravens, down the chimney.

Puff! into a chest they drop,
Full of flour up to the top.

Out they crawl from under cover
Just as white as chalk all over.

But the cracknels, precious treasure,
On a shelf they spy with pleasure.

Knacks! The chair breaks! down they go—

Schwapp!—into a trough of dough!

All enveloped now in bough,
See them, monuments of woe.

In the Baker comes, and snickers
When he sees the sugar-lickers.

One, two, three! the brats, behold!
Into two good brots are rolled.

There's the oven, all reb-hot, —
Shove 'em in as quick as thought.

Ruff! out with 'em from the heat,
They are brown anb goob to eat.

Now you think they've paid the debt!
No, my friend, they're living yet.

Knusper! Knasper! like two mice
Through their roofs they gnaw in a trice;

And the Baker cries, "You bet!
There's the rascals living yet!"
This was the bad boys' sixth trick,
But the last will follow quick.

LAST TRICK

MAX and Moritz! I grow sick,
When I think on your last trick.

Why must these two scalawags
Cut those gashes in the bags?

See! the farmer on his back
Carries corn off in a sack.

Scarce has he begun to travel,
When the corn runs out like gravel.

All at once he stops and cries:
"Darn it! I see where it lies!"

Ha! with what belighteb eyes
Max anb Moritz he espies.

Rabs! he opens wibe his sack,
Shoves the rogues in—Hukepack!

It grows warm with Max and Moritz,
For to mill the farmer hurries.

"Master Miller! Hallo, man!
Grind me that as quick as you can!"

"In with 'em!" Each wretched flopper
Headlong goes into the hopper.

As the farmer turns his back, he
Hears the mill go "creaky! Cracky!"

Here you see the bits post mortem,
Just as Fate was pleased to sort 'em.

Master Miller's bucks with speed
Gobbled up the coarse-grained feed.

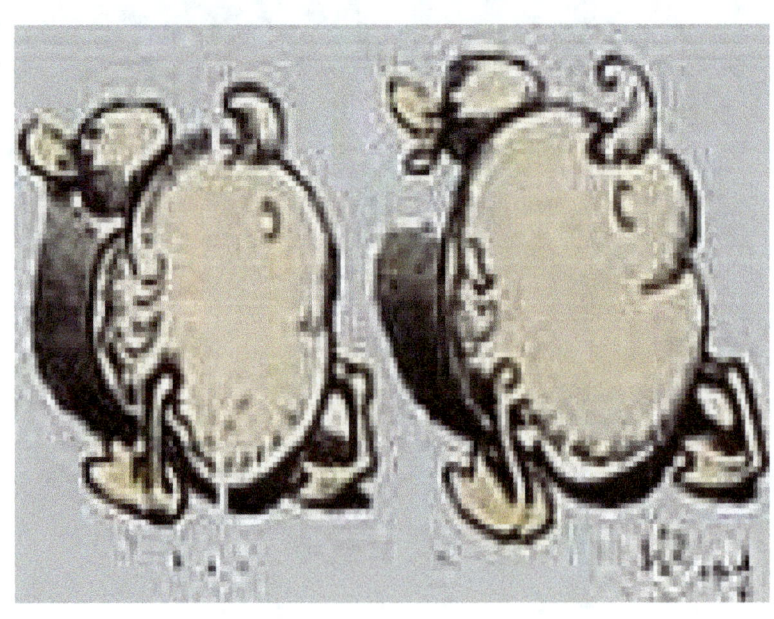

CONCLUSION.

IN the village not a word,
Not a sign, of grief, was heard.
Widow Tibbets, speaking low,
Said, "I thought it would be so!"
"None but self," cried Buck, "to blame!
Mischief is not life's true aim!"
Then said gravely Teacher Lämpel,
"There again is an example!"
"To be sure! bad thing for youth,"
Said the Baker, "a sweet tooth!"
Even Uncle says, "Good folks!
See what comes of stupid jokes!"
But the honest farmer: "Guy!
What concern is that to I?"
Through the place in short there went
One wide murmur of content:
"God be praised! the town is free
From this great rascality!"

Important Aesop's Fables

THE YOUNG CRAB AND HIS MOTHER

"Why in the world do you walk sideways like that?" said a Mother Crab to her son. "You should always walk straight forward with your toes turned out."
"Show me how to walk, mother dear," answered the little Crab obediently, "I want to learn."
So the old Crab tried and tried to walk straight forward. But she could walk sideways only, like her son. And when she wanted to turn her toes out she tripped and fell on her nose.

Do not tell others how to act unless you can set a good example.

THE SHEPHERD BOY AND THE WOLF

A Shepherd Boy tended his master's Sheep near a dark forest not far from the village. Soon he found life in the pasture very dull. All he could do to amuse himself was to talk to his dog or play on his shepherd's pipe.
One day as he sat watching the Sheep and the quiet forest, and thinking what

he would do should he see a Wolf, he thought of a plan to amuse himself.

His Master had told him to call for help should a Wolf attack the flock, and the Villagers would drive it away. So now, though he had not seen anything that even looked like a Wolf, he ran toward the village shouting at the top of his voice, "Wolf! Wolf!" As he expected, the Villagers who heard the cry dropped their work and ran in great excitement to the pasture. But when they got there they found the Boy doubled up with laughter at the trick he had played on them.

A few days later the Shepherd Boy again shouted, "Wolf! Wolf!" Again the Villagers ran to help him, only to be laughed at again.

Then one evening as the sun was setting behind the forest and the shadows were creeping out over the pasture, a Wolf really did spring from the underbrush and fall upon the Sheep.

In terror the Boy ran toward the village shouting "Wolf! Wolf!" But though the Villagers heard the cry, they did not run to help him as they had before. "He cannot fool us again," they said. The Wolf killed a great many of the Boy's sheep and then slipped away into the forest.

Liars are not believed even when they speak the truth.

THE FROGS WHO WISHED FOR A KING

The Frogs were tired of governing themselves. They had so much freedom that it had spoiled them, and they did nothing but sit around croaking in a bored manner and wishing for a government that could entertain them with the pomp and display of royalty, and rule them in a way to make them know they were being ruled. No milk and water government for them, they declared. So they sent a petition to Jupiter asking for a king.

Jupiter saw what simple and foolish creatures they were, but to keep them quiet and make them think they had a king he threw down a huge log, which fell into the water with a great splash.

The Frogs hid themselves among the reeds and grasses, thinking the new king to be some fearful giant. But they soon discovered how tame and peaceable King Log was. In a short time the younger Frogs were using him for a diving platform, while the older Frogs made him a meeting place, where they complained loudly to Jupiter about the government.

To teach the Frogs a lesson the ruler of the gods now sent a Crane to be king of Frogland. The Crane proved to be a very different sort of king from old King Log. He gobbled up the poor Frogs right and left and they soon saw what fools they had been. In mournful croaks they begged Jupiter to take away the cruel tyrant before they should all be destroyed.

"How now!" cried Jupiter "Are you not yet content? You have what you asked for and so you have only yourselves to blame for your misfortunes."

Be sure you can better your condition before you seek to change.

THE WOLF AND HIS SHADOW

A Wolf left his lair one evening in fine spirits and an excellent appetite. As he ran, the setting sun cast his shadow far out on the ground, and it looked as if the wolf were a hundred times bigger than he really was.

"Why," exclaimed the Wolf proudly, "see how big I am! Fancy me running away from a puny Lion! I'll show him who is fit to be king, he or I."

Just then an immense shadow blotted him out entirely, and the next instant a Lion struck him down with a single blow.

Do not let your fancy make you forget realities.

THE CROW AND THE PITCHER

In a spell of dry weather, when the Birds could find very little to drink, a thirsty Crow found a pitcher with a little water in it.

But the pitcher was high and had a narrow neck, and no matter how he tried, the Crow could not reach the water. The poor thing felt as if he must die of thirst.

Then an idea came to him. Picking up some small pebbles, he dropped them into the pitcher one by one. With each pebble the water rose a little higher until at last it was near enough so he could drink.

In a pinch a good use of our wits may help us out.

THE ANTS AND THE GRASSHOPPER

One bright day in late autumn a family of Ants were bustling about in the warm sunshine, drying out the grain they had stored up during the summer, when a starving Grasshopper, his fiddle under his arm, came up and humbly begged for a bite to eat.
"What!" cried the Ants in surprise, "haven't you stored anything away for the winter? What in the world were you doing all last summer?"
"I didn't have time to store up any food," whined the Grasshopper; "I was so busy making music that before I knew it the summer was gone."
The Ants shrugged their shoulders in disgust.
"Making music, were you?" they cried. "Very well; now dance!"
And they turned their backs on the Grasshopper and went on with their work.

There's a time for work and a time for play.

In the Disney version of this story, the grasshopper stays outside until winter, he manages to make it to the ants' home, they let him in and in turn he played music for them as a thanks for the shelter and food they gave him.

A RAVEN AND A SWAN

A Raven, which you know is black as coal, was envious of the Swan, because her feathers were as white as the purest snow. The foolish bird got the idea that if he lived like the Swan, swimming and diving all day long and eating the weeds and plants that grow in the water, his feathers would turn white like the Swan's.

So he left his home in the woods and fields and flew down to live on the lakes and in the marshes. But though he washed and washed all day long, almost drowning himself at it, his feathers remained as black as ever. And as the water weeds he ate did not agree with him, he got thinner and thinner, and at last he died.

A change of habits will not alter nature.

THE TWO GOATS

Two Goats, frisking gayly on the rocky steeps of a mountain valley, chanced to meet, one on each side of a deep chasm through which poured a mighty mountain torrent. The trunk of a fallen tree formed the only means of crossing the chasm, and on this not even two squirrels could have passed each other in safety. The narrow path would have made the bravest tremble. Not so our Goats. Their pride would not permit either to stand aside for the other.

One set her foot on the log. The other did likewise. In the middle they met horn to horn. Neither would give way, and so they both fell, to be swept away by the roaring torrent below.

It is better to yield than to come to misfortune through stubbornness

THE WOLF AND THE ASS

An Ass was feeding in a pasture near a wood when he saw a Wolf lurking in the shadows along the hedge. He easily guessed what the Wolf had in mind, and thought of a plan to save himself. So he pretended he was lame, and began to hobble painfully.

When the Wolf came up, he asked the Ass what had made him lame, and the Ass replied that he had stepped on a sharp thorn.

"Please pull it out," he pleaded, groaning as if in pain. "If you do not, it might stick in your throat when you eat me."

The Wolf saw the wisdom of the advice, for he wanted to enjoy his meal without any danger of choking. So the Ass lifted up his foot and the Wolf began to search very closely and carefully for the thorn.

Just then the Ass kicked out with all his might, tumbling the Wolf a dozen paces away. And while the Wolf was getting very slowly and painfully to his feet, the Ass galloped away in safety.

"Serves me right," growled the Wolf as he crept into the bushes. "I'm a butcher by trade, not a doctor."

Stick to your trade.

THE COCK AND THE FOX

One bright evening as the sun was sinking on a glorious world a wise old Cock flew into a tree to roost. Before he composed himself to rest, he flapped his wings three times and crowed loudly. But just as he was about to put his head under his wing, his beady eyes caught a flash of red and a glimpse of a long pointed nose, and there just below him stood Master Fox.

"Have you heard the wonderful news?" cried the Fox in a very joyful and excited manner.

"What news?" asked the Cock very calmly. But he had a queer, fluttery feeling inside him, for, you know, he was very much afraid of the Fox.

"Your family and mine and all other animals have agreed to forget their differences and live in peace and friendship from now on forever. Just think of it! I simply cannot wait to embrace you! Do come down, dear friend, and let us celebrate the joyful event."

"How grand!" said the Cock. "I certainly am delighted at the news." But he spoke in an absent way, and stretching up on tip toes, seemed to be looking at something afar off.

"What is it you see?" asked the Fox a little anxiously.

"Why, it looks to me like a couple of Dogs coming this way. They must have heard the good news and–"

But the Fox did not wait to hear more. Off he started on a run.

"Wait," cried the Cock. "Why do you run? The Dogs are friends of yours now!"

"Yes," answered the Fox. "But they might not have heard the news. Besides, I have a very important errand that I had almost forgotten about."

The Cock smiled as he buried his head in his feathers and went to sleep, for he had succeeded in outwitting a very crafty enemy.

The trickster is easily tricked.

THE WOLF AND THE SHEPHERD

A Wolf had been prowling around a flock of Sheep for a long time, and the Shepherd watched very anxiously to prevent him from carrying off a Lamb. But the Wolf did not try to do any harm. Instead he seemed to be helping the Shepherd take care of the Sheep. At last the Shepherd got so used to seeing the Wolf about that he forgot how wicked he could be.

One day he even went so far as to leave his flock in the Wolf's care while he went on an errand. But when he came back and saw how many of the flock had been killed and carried off, he knew how foolish to trust a Wolf.

Once a wolf, always a wolf.

THE ASTROLOGER

A man who lived a long time ago believed that he could read the future in the stars. He called himself an Astrologer, and spent his time at night gazing at the sky.
One evening he was walking along the open road outside the village. His eyes were fixed on the stars. He thought he saw there that the end of the world was at hand, when all at once, down he went into a hole full of mud and water.

There he stood up to his ears, in the muddy water, and madly clawing at the slippery sides of the hole in his effort to climb out.

His cries for help soon brought the villagers running. As they pulled him out of the mud, one of them said:
"You pretend to read the future in the stars, and yet you fail to see what is at your feet! This may teach you to pay more attention to what is right in front of you, and let the future take care of itself."
"What use is it," said another, "to read the stars, when you can't see what's right here on the earth?"

Take care of the little things and the big things will take care of themselves.

THE WOLF IN SHEEP'S CLOTHING

A certain Wolf could not get enough to eat because of the watchfulness of the Shepherds. But one night he found a sheep skin that had been cast aside and forgotten. The next day, dressed in the skin, the Wolf strolled into the pasture with the Sheep. Soon a little Lamb was following him about and was quickly led away to slaughter.
That evening the Wolf entered the fold with the flock. But it happened that the Shepherd took a fancy for mutton broth that very evening, and, picking up a knife, went to the fold. There the first he laid hands on and killed was the Wolf.

The evil doer often comes to harm through his own deceit.

THE PORCUPINE AND THE SNAKES

A Porcupine was looking for a good home. At last he found a little sheltered cave, where lived a family of Snakes. He asked them to let him share the cave with them, and the Snakes kindly consented.
The Snakes soon wished they had not given him permission to stay. His sharp quills pricked them at every turn, and at last they politely asked him to leave.

"I am very well satisfied, thank you," said the Porcupine. "I intend to stay right here." And with that, he politely escorted the Snakes out of doors. And to save their skins, the Snakes had to look for another home.

Give a finger and lose a hand.

THE MOTHER AND THE WOLF

Early one morning a hungry Wolf was prowling around a cottage at the edge of a village, when he heard a child crying in the house. Then he heard the Mother's voice say: "Hush, child, hush! Stop your crying, or I will give you to the Wolf!"
Surprised but delighted at the prospect of so delicious a meal, the Wolf settled down under an open window, expecting every moment to have the child handed out to him. But though the little one continued to fret, the Wolf waited all day in vain. Then, toward nightfall, he

151

heard the Mother's voice again as she sat down near the
window to sing and rock her baby to sleep.
"There, child, there! The Wolf shall not get you. No, no! Daddy
is watching and Daddy will kill him if he should come near!"
Just then the Father came within sight of the home, and the
Wolf was barely able to save himself from the Dogs by a clever
bit of running.

Do not believe everything you hear.

THE FLIES AND THE HONEY

A jar of honey was upset and the sticky sweetness flowed out
on the table. The sweet smell of the honey soon brought a
large number of Flies buzzing around. They did not wait for an
invitation. No, indeed; they settled right down, feet and all, to
gorge themselves. The Flies were quickly smeared from head
to foot with honey. Their wings stuck together. They could not
pull their feet out of the sticky mass. And so they died, giving
their lives for the sake of a taste of sweetness.

Be not greedy for a little passing pleasure. It may destroy you.

THE DOG AND HIS REFLECTION

A Dog, to whom the butcher had
thrown a bone, was hurrying
home with his prize as fast as he
could go. As he crossed a
narrow footbridge, he happened
to look down and saw himself
reflected in the quiet water as if
in a mirror. But the greedy Dog

152

thought he saw a real Dog carrying a bone much bigger than his own.

If he had stopped to think he would have known better. But instead of thinking, he dropped his bone and sprang at the Dog in the river, only to find himself swimming for dear life to reach the shore. At last he managed to scramble out, and as he stood sadly thinking about the good bone he had lost, he realized what a stupid Dog he had been.

It is very foolish to be greedy

THE HARE AND THE TORTOISE

A Hare was making fun of the Tortoise one day for being so slow.

"Do you ever get anywhere?" he asked with a mocking laugh. "Yes," replied the Tortoise, "and I get there sooner than you think. I'll run you a race and prove it." The Hare was much amused at the idea of running a race with the Tortoise, but for the fun of the thing he agreed. So the Fox, who had consented to act as judge, marked the distance and started the runners off.

The Hare was soon far out of sight, and to make the Tortoise feel very deeply how ridiculous it was for him to try a race with a Hare, he lay down beside the course to take a nap until the Tortoise should catch up.

The Tortoise meanwhile kept going slowly but steadily, and, after a time, passed the place where the Hare was sleeping. But the Hare slept on very peacefully; and when at last he did wake up, the Tortoise was near the goal. The Hare now ran his swiftest, but he could not overtake the Tortoise in time.

The race is not always to the swift.

THE FOX AND THE CROW

One bright morning as the Fox was following his sharp nose through the wood in search of a bite to eat, he saw a Crow on the limb of a tree overhead. This was by no means the first Crow the Fox had ever seen. What caught his attention this time and made him stop for a second look, was that the lucky Crow held a bit of cheese in her beak. "No need to search any farther," thought sly Master Fox. "Here is a dainty bite for my breakfast."

Up he trotted to the foot of the tree in which the Crow was sitting, and looking up admiringly, he cried, "Good-morning, beautiful creature!"

The Crow, her head cocked on one side, watched the Fox suspiciously. But she kept her beak tightly closed on the cheese and did not return his greeting.

"What a charming creature she is!" said the Fox. "How her feathers shine! What a beautiful form and what splendid wings!

Such a wonderful Bird should have a very lovely voice, since everything else about her is so perfect. Could she sing just one song, I know I should hail her Queen of Birds."

Listening to these flattering words, the Crow forgot all her suspicion, and also her breakfast. She wanted very much to be called Queen of Birds.

So she opened her beak wide to utter her loudest caw, and down fell the cheese straight into the Fox's open mouth.

"Thank you," said Master Fox sweetly, as he walked off. "Though it is cracked, you have a voice sure enough. But where are your wits?"

The flatterer lives at the expense of those who will listen to him.

THE FIGHTING COCKS AND THE EAGLE

Once there were two Cocks living in the same farmyard who could not bear the sight of each other. At last one day they flew up to fight it out, beak and claw. They fought until one of them was beaten and crawled off to a corner to hide.

The Cock that had won the battle flew to the top of the hen-house, and, proudly flapping his wings, crowed with all his might to tell the world about his victory. But an Eagle, circling overhead, heard the boasting chanticleer and, swooping down, carried him off to his nest.

His rival saw the deed, and coming out of his corner, took his place as master of the farmyard.

Pride goes before a fall.

Important Brother Grimm Stories for All Kids

The Story of the Youth Who Went Forth to Learn What Fear Was

A certain father had two sons, the elder of whom was smart and sensible, and could do everything, but the younger was stupid and could neither learn nor understand anything.

And when people saw him they said, "There's a fellow who will give his father some trouble!"

When anything had to be done, it was always the elder who was forced to do it; but if his father bade him fetch anything when it was late, or in the night-time, and the way led through the churchyard, or any other dismal place, he answered: "Oh, no, father, I'll not go there, it makes me shudder!" for he was afraid.

Or when stories were told by the fire at night which made the flesh creep, the listeners sometimes said: "Oh, it makes us shudder!"

The younger sat in a corner and listened with the rest of them, and could not imagine what they could mean. "They are always saying, it makes me shudder, it makes me shudder!' It does not make me shudder," thought he. "That, too, must be an art of which I understand nothing."

Now it came to pass that his father said to him one day: "Hearken to me, thou fellow in the corner there, thou art growing tall and strong, and thou too must learn something by which thou canst earn thy living. Look how thy brother works, but thou dost not even earn thy salt."

"Well, father," he replied, "I am quite willing to learn something– indeed, if it could but be managed, I should like to learn how to shudder. I don't understand that at all yet."
The elder brother smiled when he heard that, and thought to himself, "Good God, what a blockhead that brother of mine is! He will never be good for anything as long as he lives. He who wants to be a sickle must bend himself betimes."

The father sighed, and answered him "thou shalt soon learn what it is to shudder, but thou wilt not earn thy bread by that."
Soon after this the sexton came to the house on a visit, and the father bewailed his trouble, and told him how his younger son was so backward in every respect that he knew nothing and learnt nothing. "Just think," said he, "when I asked him how he was going to earn his bread, he actually wanted to learn to shudder." "If that be all," replied the sexton, "he can learn that with me. Send him to me, and I will soon polish him." The father was glad to do it, for he thought, "It will train the boy a little." The sexton therefore took him into his house, and he had to ring the bell. After a day or two, the sexton awoke him at midnight, and bade him arise and go up into the church tower and ring the bell. "Thou shalt soon learn what shuddering is," thought he, and secretly went there before him; and when the boy was at the top of the tower and turned round, and was just going to take hold of the bell rope, he saw a white figure standing on the stairs opposite the sounding hole. "Who is there?" cried he, but the figure made no reply, and did not move or stir. "Give an answer," cried the boy, "or take thyself off, thou hast no business here at night."

The sexton, however, remained standing motionless that the boy might think he was a ghost. The boy cried a second time, "What do you want here?–speak if thou art an honest fellow, or I will throw thee down the steps!" The sexton thought, "he can't intend to be as bad as his words," uttered no sound and stood as if he were made of stone. Then the boy called to him for the third time, and as that was also to no purpose, he ran against him and pushed the ghost down the stairs, so that it fell down ten steps and remained lying there in a corner. There upon he rang the bell, went home, and without saying a word went to bed, and fell asleep. The sexton's wife waited a long time for her husband, but he did not come back. At length she became uneasy, and wakened the boy, and asked, "Dost thou not know where my husband is? He climbed up the tower before thou didst." "No, I don't know," replied the boy, "but some one was standing by the sounding hole on the other side of the steps, and as he would neither give an answer nor go away, I took him for a scoundrel, and threw him downstairs, just go there and you will see if it was he. I should be sorry if it were." The woman ran away and found her husband, who was lying moaning in the corner, and had broken his leg.

She carried him down, and then with loud screams she hastened to the boy's father. "Your boy," cried she, "has been the cause of a great misfortune! He has thrown my husband down the steps and made him break his leg. Take the good-for-nothing fellow away from our house." The father was terrified, and ran thither and scolded the boy. "What wicked tricks are these?" said he, "the devil must have put this into thy head." "Father," he replied, "do listen to me. I am quite innocent. He was standing there by night like one who is intending to do some evil. I did not know who it was, and I entreated him three times either to speak or to go away." "Ah," said the father, "I have nothing but unhappiness with you. Go out of my sight. I will see thee no more."

"Yes, father, right willingly, wait only until it is day. Then will I go forth and learn how to shudder, and then I shall, at any rate, understand one art which will support me." "Learn what thou wilt," spake the father, "it is all the same to me. Here are fifty thalers for thee. Take these and go into the wide world, and tell no one from whence thou comest, and who is thy father, for I have reason to be ashamed of thee." "Yes, father, it shall be as you will. If you desire nothing more than that, I can easily keep it in mind."

When day dawned, therefore, the boy put his fifty thalers into his pocket, and went forth on the great highway, and continually said to himself, "If I could but shudder! If I could but shudder!" Then a man approached who heard this conversation which the youth was holding with himself, and when they had walked a little farther to where they could see the gallows, the man said to him, "Look, there is the tree where seven men have married the ropemaker's daughter, and are now learning how to fly. Sit down below it, and wait till night comes, and you will soon learn how to shudder." "If that is all that is wanted," answered the youth, "it is easily done; but if I learn how to shudder as fast as that, thou shalt have my fifty thalers. Just come back to me early in the morning." Then the youth went to the gallows, sat down below it, and waited till evening came. And as he was cold, he lighted himself a fire, but at midnight the wind blew so sharply that in spite of his fire, he could not get warm. And as the wind knocked the hanged men against each other, and they moved backwards and forwards, he thought to himself "Thou shiverest below by the fire, but how those up above must freeze and suffer!" And as he felt pity for them, he raised the ladder, and climbed up, unbound one of them after the other, and brought down all seven. Then he stirred the fire, blew it, and set them all round it to warm themselves. But they sat there and did not stir, and the fire caught their clothes. So he said, "Take care, or I will hang you up again." The dead men, however, did not hear, but were quite silent, and let their rags go on burning. On this he grew angry, and said, "If you will not take care, I cannot help you, I will not be burnt with you," and he hung them up again each in his turn. Then he sat down by his fire and fell asleep, and the next morning the man came to him and wanted to have the fifty thalers, and said, "Well, dost thou know how to shudder?" "No," answered he, "how was I to get to know? Those fellows up there did not open their mouths, and were so stupid that

they let the few old rags which they had on their bodies get burnt."
Then the man saw that he would not get the fifty thalers that day,and
went away saying, "One of this kind has never come my way before."
The youth likewise went his way, and once more began to mutter to
himself, "Ah, if I could but shudder! Ah, if I could but shudder!" A
waggoner who was striding behind him heard that and asked, "Who
are you?" "I don't know," answered the youth. Then the waggoner
asked, "From whence comest thou?" "I know not." "Who is thy
father?" "That I may not tell thee." "What is it that thou art always
muttering between thy teeth." "Ah," replied the youth, "I do so wish I
could shudder, but no one can teach me how to do it." "Give up thy
foolish chatter," said the waggoner. "Come, go with me, I will see
about a place for thee." The youth went with the waggoner, and in
the evening they arrived at an inn where they wished to pass the
night. Then at the entrance of the room the youth again said quite
loudly, "If I could but shudder! If I could but shudder!" The host who
heard this, laughed and said, "If that is your desire, there ought to be
a good opportunity for you here.""Ah, be silent," said the hostess, "so
many inquisitive persons have already lost their lives, it would be a
pity and a shame if such beautiful eyes as these should never see the
daylight again."
But the youth said, "However difficult it may be, I will learn it and for
this purpose indeed have I journeyed forth." He let the host have no
rest, until the latter told him, that not far from thence stood a haunted
castle where any one could very easily learn what shuddering was, if
he would but watch in it for three nights. The King had promised that
he who would venture should have his daughter to wife, and she was
the most beautiful maiden the sun shone on. Great treasures likewise
lay in the castle, which were guarded by evil spirits, and these
treasures would then be freed,and would make a poor man rich
enough. Already many men had gone into the castle, but as yet none
had come out again. Then the youth went next morning to the King
and said if he were allowed he would watch three nights in the
haunted castle. The King looked at him, and as the youth pleased
him, he said, "Thou mayest ask for three things to take into the castle
with thee, but they must be things without life." Then he answered,
"Then I ask for a fire, a turning lathe, and a cutting-board with the
knife." The King had these things carried into the castle for him
during the day. When night was drawing near, the youth went up
and made himself a bright fire in one of the rooms, placed the
cutting-board and knife beside it, and seated himself by the turning-
lathe. "Ah, if I could but shudder!" said he, "but I shall not learn it
here either." Towards midnight he was about to poke his fire, and as
he was blowing it, something cried suddenly from one corner, "Au,

miau! how cold we are!" "You simpletons!" cried he, "what are you crying about? If you are cold, come and take a seat by the fire and warm yourselves." And when he had said that, two great black cats came with one tremendous leap and sat down on each side of him, and looked savagely at him with their fiery eyes. After a short time, when they had warmed themselves, they said, "Comrade, shall we have a game at cards?" "Why not?" he replied, "but just show me your paws." Then they stretched out their claws. "Oh," said he, "what long nails you have! Wait, I must first cut them for you." There upon he seized them by the throats, put them on the cutting-board and screwed their feet fast. "I have looked at your fingers," said he, "and my fancy for card-playing has gone," and he struck them dead and threw them out into the water. But when he had made away with these two, and was about to sit down again by his fire, out from every hole and corner came black cats and black dogs with red-hot chains, and more and more of them came until he could no longer stir, and they yelled horribly, and got on his fire, pulled it to pieces, and tried to put it out. He watched them for a while quietly, but at last when they were going too far, he seized his cutting-knife, and cried, "Away with ye, vermin," and began to cut them down. Part of them ran away, the others he killed, and threw out into the fish-pond. When he came back he fanned the embers of his fire again and warmed himself. And as he thus sat, his eyes would keep open no longer, and he felt a desire to sleep. Then he looked round and saw a great bed in the corner. "That is the very thing for me," said he, and got into it. When he was just going to shut his eyes, however, the bed began to move of its own accord, and went over the whole of the castle. "That's right," said he, "but go faster." Then the bed rolled on as if six horses were harnessed to it, up and down, over thresholds and steps, but suddenly hop, hop, it turned over upside down, and lay on him like a mountain. But he threw quilts and pillows up in the air, got out and said, "Now any one who likes, may drive," and lay down by his fire, and slept till it was day. In the morning the King came, and when he saw him lying there on the ground, he thought the evil spirits had killed him and he was dead. Then said he, "After all it is a pity,–he is a handsome man." The youth heard it, got up, and said, "It has not come to that yet." Then the King was astonished, but very glad, and asked how he had fared. "Very well indeed," answered he; "one night is past, the two others will get over likewise." Then he went to the innkeeper, who opened his eyes very wide, and said, "I never expected to see thee alive again! Hast thou learnt how to shudder yet?" "No," said he, "it is all in vain. If some one would but tell me."

The second night he again went up into the old castle, sat down by the fire, and once more began his old song, "If I could but shudder." When midnight came, an uproar and noise of tumbling about was heard; at first it was low, but it grew louder and louder. Then it was quiet for a while, and at length with a loud scream, half a man came down the chimney and fell before him. "Hollo!" cried he, "another half belongs to this. This is too little!" Then the uproar began again, there was a roaring and howling, and the other half fell down likewise. "Wait," said he, "I will just blow up the fire a little for thee." When he had done that and looked round again, the two pieces were joined together, and a frightful man was sitting in his place. "That is no part of our bargain," said the youth, "the bench is mine." The man wanted to push him away; the youth, however, would not allow that, but thrust him off with all his strength, and seated himself again in his own place. Then still more men fell down, one after the other; they brought nine dead men's legs and two skulls, and set them up and played at nine-pins with them. The youth also wanted to play and said "Hark you, can I join you?" "Yes, if thou hast any money." "Money enough," replied he, "but your balls are not quite round."

Then he took the skulls and put them in the lathe and turned them till they were round. "There, now, they will roll better!" said he. "Hurrah! Now it goes merrily!" He played with them and lost some of his money, but when it struck twelve, everything vanished from his sight. He lay down and quietly fell asleep. Next morning the King came to inquire after him. "How has it fared with you this time?" asked he. "I have been playing at nine-pins," he answered, "and have lost a couple of farthings." "Hast thou not shuddered then?" "Eh, what?"

said he, "I have made merry. If I did but know what it was to shudder!"

The third night he sat down again on his bench and said quite sadly, "If I could but shudder." When it grew late, six tall men came in and brought a coffin. Then said he, "Ha, ha, that is certainly my little cousin, who died only a few days ago," and he beckoned with his finger, and cried "Come, little cousin, come." They placed the coffin on the ground, but he went to it and took the lid off, and a dead man lay therein. He felt his face, but it was cold as ice. "Stop," said he, "I will warm thee a little," and went to the fire and warmed his hand and laid it on the dead man's face, but he remained cold. Then he took him out, and sat down by the fire and laid him on his breast and rubbed his arms that the blood might circulate again. As this also did no good, he thought to himself "When two people lie in bed together, they warm each other," and carried him to the bed, covered him over and lay down by him. After a short time the dead man became warm too, and began to move. Then said the youth, "See, little cousin, have I not warmed thee?" The dead man, however, got up and cried, "Now will I strangle thee."

"What!" said he, "is that the way thou thankest me? Thou shalt at once go into thy coffin again," and he took him up, threw him into it, and shut the lid. Then came the six men and carried him away again. "I cannot manage to shudder," said he. "I shall never learn it here as long as I live."

Then a man entered who was taller than all others, and looked terrible. He was old, however, and had a long white beard. "Thou wretch," cried he, "thou shalt soon learn what it is to shudder, for thou shalt die." "Not so fast," replied the youth. "If I am to die, I shall have to have a say in it." "I will soon seize thee," said the fiend. "Softly, softly, do not talk so big. I am as strong as thou art, and perhaps even stronger." "We shall see," said the old man. "If thou art stronger, I will let thee go—come, we will try." Then he led him by dark passages to a smith's forge, took an axe, and with one blow struck an anvil into the ground. "I can do better than that," said the youth, and went to the other anvil. The old man placed himself near and wanted to look on, and his white beard hung down. Then the youth seized the axe, split the anvil with one blow, and struck the old man's beard in with it. "Now I have thee," said the youth. "Now it is thou who will have to die." Then he seized an iron bar and beat the old man till he moaned and entreated him to stop, and he would give him great riches. The youth drew out the axe and let him go. The old man led him back into the castle, and in a cellar showed him three chests full of gold. "Of these," said he, "one part is for the poor, the other for the king, the third is thine." In the meantime it struck twelve,

and the spirit disappeared; the youth, therefore, was left in darkness.
"I shall still be able to find my way out," said he, and felt about,
found the way into the room, and slept there by his fire. Next morning
the King came and said "Now thou must have learnt what shuddering
is?" "No," he answered; "what can it be? My dead cousin was here,
and a bearded man came and showed me a great deal of money
down below, but no one told me what it was to shudder." "Then,"
said the King, "thou hast delivered the castle, and shalt marry my
daughter." "That is all very well," said he, "but still I do not know
what it is to shudder."

Then the gold was brought up and the wedding celebrated; but
howsoever much the young king loved his wife, and however happy
he was, he still said always "If I could but shudder–if I could but
shudder." And at last she (his wife) was angry at this. Her waiting-
maid said, "I will find a cure for him; he shall soon learn what it is to
shudder." She went out to the stream which flowed through the
garden, and had a whole bucketful of gudgeons brought to her. At
night when the young king was sleeping, his wife was to draw the
clothes off him and empty the bucketful of cold water with the
gudgeons in it over him, so that the little fishes would sprawl about
him. When this was done, he woke up and cried "Oh, what makes me
shudder so?–what makes me shudder so, dear wife? Ah! now I know
what it is to shudder!"

The Wolf and the Seven Little Kids

There was once upon a time an old goat who had seven little kids, and loved them with all the love of a mother for her children. One day she wanted to go into the forest and fetch some food. So she called all seven to her and said, "Dear children, I have to go into the forest, be on your guard against the wolf; if he come in, he will devour you all–skin, hair, and all. The wretch often disguises himself, but you will know him at once by his rough voice and his black feet."

The kids said, "Dear mother, we will take good care of ourselves; you may go away without any anxiety." Then the old one bleated, and went on her way with an easy mind.
It was not long before some one knocked at the house-door and called, "Open the door, dear children; your mother is here, and has brought something back with her for each of you."

But the little kids knew that it was the wolf, by the rough voice; "We will not open the door," cried they, "thou art not our mother. She has a soft, pleasant voice, but thy voice is rough; thou art the wolf!" Then the wolf went away to a shopkeeper and bought himself a great lump of chalk, ate this and made his voice soft with it. The he came back, knocked at the door of the house, and cried,

"Open the door, dear children, your mother is here and has brought something back with her for each of you." But the wolf had laid his black paws against the window, and the children saw them and cried, "We will not open the door, our mother has not black feet like thee; thou art the wolf." Then the wolf ran to a baker and said, "I have hurt my feet, rub some dough over them for me." And when the baker had rubbed his feet over, he ran to the miller and said, "Strew some white meal over my feet for me." The miller thought to himself, "The wolf wants to deceive someone," and refused; but the wolf said, "If thou wilt not do it, I will devour thee." Then the miller was afraid, and made his paws white for him. Truly, this is the way of mankind.

So now the wretch went for the third time to the house-door, knocked at it and said, "Open the door for me, children, your dear little mother has come home, and has brought every one of you something back from the forest with her." The little kids cried, "First show us thy paws that we may know if thou art our dear little mother." Then he put his paws in through the window, and when the kids saw that they were white, they believed that all he said was true, and opened the door. But who should come in but the wolf! They were terrified and wanted to hide themselves. One sprang under the table, the second into the bed, the third into the stove, the fourth into the kitchen, the fifth into the cupboard, the sixth under the washing-bowl, and the seventh into the clock-case. But the wolf found them all, and used no great ceremony; one after the other he swallowed them down his throat. The youngest, who was in the clock-case, was the only one he did not find. When the wolf had satisfied his appetite he took himself off, laid himself down under a tree in the green meadow outside, and began to sleep. Soon afterwards the old goat came home again from the forest. Ah! What a sight she saw there! The house-door stood wide open. The table, chairs, and benches were thrown down, the washing-bowl lay broken to pieces, and the quilts and pillows were pulled off the bed. She sought her children, but they were nowhere to be found. She called them one after another by name, but no one answered. At last, when she came to the youngest, a soft voice cried, "Dear mother, I am in the clock-case." She took the kid out, and it told her that the wolf had come and had eaten all the others. Then you may imagine how she wept over her poor children.

At length in her grief she went out, and the youngest kid ran with her. When they came to the meadow, there lay the wolf by the tree and snored so loud that the branches shook. She looked at him on every side and saw that something was moving and struggling in his gorged belly. "Ah, heavens," said she, "is it possible that my poor children whom he has swallowed down for his supper, can be still alive?"

Then the kid had to run home and fetch scissors, and a needle and thread, and the goat cut open the monster's stomach, and hardly had she make one cut, than one little kid thrust its head out, and when she cut farther, all six sprang out one after another, and were all still alive, and had suffered no injury whatever, for in his greediness the monster had swallowed them down whole. What rejoicing there was! They embraced their dear mother, and jumped like a sailor at his wedding. The mother, however, said, "Now go and look for some big stones, and we will fill the wicked beast's stomach with them while he is still asleep." Then the seven kids dragged the stones thither with all speed, and put as many of them into his stomach as they could get in; and the mother sewed him up again in the greatest haste, so that he was not aware of anything and never once stirred.

When the wolf at length had had his sleep out, he got on his legs, and as the stones in his stomach made him very thirsty, he wanted to go to a well to drink. But when he began to walk and move about, the stones in his stomach knocked against each other and rattled. Then cried he,

"What rumbles and tumbles against my poor bones? I thought 't was six kids, but it's naught but big stones."

And when he got to the well and stooped over the water and was just about to drink, the heavy stones made him fall in, and there was no help, so he had to drown miserably. When the seven kids saw that, they came running to the spot and cried aloud, "The wolf is dead! The wolf is dead!" and danced for joy round about the well with their mother.

Little Red-Cap (Red Riding Hood)

Once upon a time there was a dear little girl who was loved by every one who looked at her, but most of all by her grandmother, and there was nothing that she would not have given to the child. Once she gave her a little cap of red velvet, which suited her so well that she would never wear anything else; so she was always called "Little Red-Cap."

One day her mother said to her, "Come, Little Red-Cap, here is a piece of cake and a bottle of wine; take them to your grandmother, she is ill and weak, and they will do her good. Set out before it gets hot, and when you are going, walk nicely and quietly and do not run off the path, or you may fall and break the bottle, and then your grandmother will get nothing; and when you go into her room, don't forget to say, 'Good-morning,' and don't peep into every corner before you do it."

"I will take great care," said Little Red-Cap to her mother, and gave her hand on it.

The grandmother lived out in the wood, half a league from the village, and just as Little Red-Cap entered the wood, a wolf met her. Red-Cap did not know what a wicked creature he was, and was not at all afraid of him.

"Good-day, Little Red-Cap," said he.
"Thank you kindly, wolf."
"Whither away so early, Little Red-Cap?"
"To my grandmother's."
"What have you got in your apron?"
"Cake and wine; yesterday was baking-day, so poor sick grandmother is to have something good, to make her stronger."
"Where does your grandmother live, Little Red-Cap?"
"A good quarter of a league farther on in the wood; her house stands under the three large oak-trees, the nut-trees are just below; you surely must know it," replied Little Red-Cap.

The wolf thought to himself, "What a tender young creature! what a nice plump mouthful–she will be better to eat than the old woman. I must act craftily, so as to catch both." So he walked for a short time by the side of Little Red-Cap, and then he said, "See Little Red-Cap, how pretty the flowers are about here–why do you not look round? I believe, too, that you do not hear how sweetly the little birds are singing; you walk gravely along as if you were going to school, while everything else out here in the wood is merry."

Little Red-Cap raised her eyes, and when she saw the sunbeams dancing here and there through the trees, and pretty flowers growing everywhere, she thought, "Suppose I take grandmother afresh nosegay; that would please her too. It is so early in the day that I shall still get there in good time;" and so she ran from the path into the wood to look for flowers. And whenever she handpicked one, she fancied that she saw a still prettier one farther on, and ran after it, and so got deeper and deeper into the wood.

Meanwhile the wolf ran straight to the grandmother's house and knocked at the door.

"Who is there?"

"Little Red-Cap," replied the wolf. "She is bringing cake and wine; open the door."

"Lift the latch," called out the grandmother, "I am too weak, and cannot get up."

The wolf lifted the latch, the door flew open, and without saying a word he went straight to the grandmother's bed, and devoured her. Then he put on her clothes, dressed himself in her cap, laid himself in bed and drew the curtains.

Little Red-Cap, however, had been running about picking flowers, and when she had gathered so many that she could carry no more, she remembered her grandmother, and set out on the way to her. She was surprised to find the cottage-door standing open, and when she went into the room, she had such a strange feeling that she said to herself, "Oh dear! how uneasy I feel to-day, and at other times I like being with grandmother so much." She called out, "Good morning," but received no answer; so she went to the bed and drew back the curtains. There lay her grandmother with her cap pulled far over her face, and looking very strange.

"Oh! grandmother," she said, "what big ears you have!"

"The better to hear you with, my child," was the reply.

"But, grandmother, what big eyes you have!" she said.

"The better to see you with, my dear."

"But, grandmother, what large hands you have!"

"The better to hug you with."

"Oh! but, grandmother, what a terrible big mouth you have!"

"The better to eat you with!"

And scarcely had the wolf said this, than with one bound he was out of bed and swallowed up Red-Cap.

When the wolf had appeased his appetite, he lay down again in the bed, fell asleep and began to snore very loud. The huntsman was just passing the house, and thought to himself, "How the old woman is snoring! I must just see if she wants anything." So he went into the room, and when he came to the bed, he saw that the wolf was lying in it. "Do I find thee here, thou old sinner!" said he. "I have long sought thee!" Then just as he was going to fire at him, it occurred to him that the wolf might have devoured the grandmother, and that she might still be saved, so he did not fire, but took a pair of scissors, and began to cut open the stomach of the sleeping wolf. When he had made two snips, he saw the little Red-Cap shining, and then he made two snips more, and the little girl sprang out, crying, "Ah, how frightened I have been! How dark it was inside the wolf;" and after that the aged grandmother came out alive also, but scarcely able to breathe. Red-Cap, however, quickly fetched great stones with which they filled the wolf's body, and when he awoke, he wanted to run away, but the stones were so heavy that he fell down at once, and fell dead.

Then all three were delighted. The huntsman drew off the wolf's skin and went home with it; the grandmother ate the cake and drank the wine which Red-Cap had brought, and revived, but Red-Cap thought to herself, "As long as I live, I will never by myself leave the path, to run into the wood, when my mother has forbidden me to do so."

* * * * * * *

It is also related that once when Red-Cap was again taking cakes to the old grandmother, another wolf spoke to her, and tried to entice her from the path. Red-Cap, however, was on her guard, and went straight forward on her way, and told her grandmother that she had met the wolf, and that he had said "good-morning" to her, but with such a wicked look in his eyes, that if they had not been on the public road she was certain he would have eaten her up. "Well," said the grandmother, "we will shut the door, that he may not come in." Soon afterwards the wolf knocked, and cried, "Open the door, grandmother, I am little Red-Cap, and am fetching you some cakes." But they did not speak, or open the door, so the grey-beard stole twice or thrice round the house, and at last jumped on the roof, intending to wait until Red-Cap went home in the evening, and then to steal after her and devour her in the darkness. But the grandmother saw what was in his thoughts. In front of the house was a great stone trough, so she said to the child, "Take the pail, Red-Cap; I made some sausages yesterday, so carry the water in which I boiled them to the trough." Red-Cap carried until the great trough was quite full. Then the smell of the sausages reached the wolf, and he sniffed and peeped down, and at last stretched out his neck so far that he could no longer keep his footing and began to slip, and slipped down from the roof straight into the great trough, and was drowned. But Red-Cap went joyously home, and never did anything to harm anyone.

Hansel and Gretel

ard by a great forest dwelt a poor wood-cutter with his wife
and his two children. The boy was called Hansel and the girl Gretel.
He had little to bite and to break, and once when great scarcity fell
on the land, he could no longer procure daily bread. Now when he
thought over this by night in his bed, and tossed about in his anxiety,
he groaned and said to his wife, "What is to become of us? How are
we to feed our poor children, when we no longer have anything even
for ourselves?" "I'll tell you what, husband," answered the woman,
"Early tomorrow morning we will take the children out into the forest
to where it is the thickest, there we will light a fire for them, and give
each of them one piece of bread more, and then we will go to our
work and leave them alone. They will not find the way home again,
and we shall be rid of them." "No, wife," said the man, "I will not do
that; how can I bear to leave my children alone in the forest?–the
wild animals would soon come and tear them to pieces." "O, thou
fool!" said she, "Then we must all four die of hunger, thou mayest as
well plane the planks for our coffins," and she left him no peace until
he consented. "But I feel very sorry for the poor children, all the
same," said the man.

The two children had also not been able to sleep for hunger, and had
heard what their step-mother had said to their father. Gretel wept
bitter tears, and said to Hansel, "Now all is over with us.""Be quiet,
Gretel," said Hansel, "do not distress thyself, I will soon find a way to
help us." And when the old folks had fallen asleep, he got up, put on
his little coat, opened the door below, and crept outside. The moon
shone brightly, and the white pebbles which lay in front of the house
glittered like real silver pennies. Hansel stooped and put as many of
them in the little pocket of his coat as he could possibly get in. Then
he went back and said to Gretel, "Be comforted, dear little sister, and
sleep in peace, God will not forsake us," and he lay down again in
his bed. When day dawned, but before the sun had risen, the woman
came and awoke the two children, saying "Get up, you sluggards! we
are going into the forest to fetch wood." She gave each a little piece
of bread, and said, "There is something for your dinner, but do not
eat it up before then, for you will get nothing else." Gretel took the
bread under her apron, as Hansel had the stones in his pocket. Then
they all set out together on the way to the forest. When they had
walked a short time, Hansel stood still and peeped back at the

house, and did so again and again. His father said, "Hansel, what art thou looking at there and staying behind for? Mind what thou art about, and do not forget how to use thy legs." "Ah, father," said Hansel, "I am looking at my little white cat, which is sitting up on the roof, and wants to say good-bye to me." The wife said, "Fool, that is not thy little cat, that is the morning sun which is shining on the chimneys." Hansel, however, had not been looking back at the cat, but had been constantly throwing one of the white pebble-stones out of his pocket on the road.

When they had reached the middle of the forest, the father said,"Now, children, pile up some wood, and I will light a fire that you may not be cold." Hansel and Gretel gathered brushwood together, as high as a little hill. The brushwood was lighted, and when the flames were burning very high, the woman said, "Now, children, lay yourselves down by the fire and rest, we will go into the forest and cut some wood. When we have done, we will come back and fetch you away."

Hansel and Gretel sat by the fire, and when noon came, each ate a little piece of bread, and as they heard the strokes of the wood-axe they believed that their father was near. It was not, however, the axe, it was a branch which he had fastened to a withered tree which the wind was blowing backwards and forwards. And as they had been sitting such a long time, their eyes shut with fatigue, and they fell fast asleep. When at last they awoke, it was already dark night. Gretel began to cry and said,"How are we to get out of the forest now?" But Hansel comforted her and said, "Just wait a little, until the moon has risen, and then we will soon find the way." And when the full moon had risen, Hansel took his little sister by the hand, and followed the pebbles which shone like newly-coined silver pieces, and showed them the way.

They walked the whole night long, and by break of day came once more to their father's house. They knocked at the door, and when the woman opened it and saw that it was Hansel and Gretel,she said, "You naughty children, why have you slept so long in the forest?–we thought you were never coming back at all!" The father, however, rejoiced, for it had cut him to the heart to leave them behind alone. Not long afterwards, there was once more great scarcity in all parts, and the children heard their mother saying at night to their father, "Everything is eaten again, we have one half loaf left, and after that there is an end. The children must go, we will take them farther into the wood, so that they will not find their way out again; there is no other means of saving ourselves!" The man's heart was heavy, and he thought "it would be better for thee to share the last mouthful with thy children." The woman, however, would listen to nothing that he had to say, but scolded and reproached him. He who says A must say B, likewise, and as he had yielded the first time, he had to do so a second time also.

The children were, however, still awake and had heard the conversation. When the old folks were asleep, Hansel again got up, and wanted to go out and pick up pebbles as he had done before, but the woman had locked the door, and Hansel could not get out. Nevertheless he comforted his little sister, and said, "Do not cry, Gretel, go to sleep quietly, the good God will help us."

Early in the morning came the woman, and took the children out of their beds. Their bit of bread was given to them, but it was still smaller than the time before. On the way into the forest Hansel crumbled his in his pocket, and often stood still and threw a morsel on the ground. "Hansel, why dost thou stop and look round?" said the father, "go on." "I am looking back at my little pigeon which is sitting on the roof, and wants to say goodbye to me," answered Hansel. "Simpleton!" said the woman, "that is not thy little pigeon, that is the morning sun that is shining on the chimney." Hansel, however, little by little, threw all the crumbs on the path.

The woman led the children still deeper into the forest, where they had never in their lives been before. Then a great fire was again made, and the mother said, "Just sit there, you children, and when you are tired you may sleep a little; we are going into the forest to cut wood, and in the evening when we are done, we will come and fetch you away." When it was noon, Gretel shared her piece of bread with Hansel, who had scattered his by the way. Then they fell asleep and evening came and went, but no one came to the poor children. They did not awake until it was dark night, and Hansel comforted his little sister and said, "Just wait, Gretel, until the moon rises, and then we shall see the crumbs of bread which I have strewn about, they will show us our way home again." When the moon came they set out, but they found no crumbs, for the many thousands of birds which fly about in the woods and fields had picked them all up. Hansel said to Gretel, "We shall soon find the way," but they did not find it. They walked the whole night and all the next day too from morning till evening, but they did not get out of the forest, and were very hungry, for they had nothing to eat but two or three berries, which grew on the ground. And as they were so weary that their legs would carry them no longer, they lay down beneath a tree and fell asleep.

It was now three mornings since they had left their father's house. They began to walk again, but they always got deeper into the forest, and if help did not come soon, they must die of hunger and weariness. When it was mid-day, they saw a beautiful snow-white bird sitting on a bough, which sang so delightfully that they stood still and listened to it.

And when it had finished its song, it spread its wings and flew away before them, and they followed it until they reached a little house, on the roof of which it alighted; and when they came quite up to the little house they saw that it was built of bread and covered with cakes, but that the windows were of clear sugar. "We will set to work on that," said Hansel, "and have a good meal. I will eat a bit of the roof, and thou, Gretel, canst eat some of the window, it will taste sweet." Hansel reached up above, and broke off a little of the roof to try how it tasted, and Gretel leant against the window and nibbled at the panes. Then as oft voice cried from the room,
"Nibble, nibble, gnaw, Who is nibbling at my little house?"
The children answered,

"The wind, the wind, The heaven-born wind," and went on eating without disturbing themselves. Hansel, who thought the roof tasted very nice, tore down a great piece of it, and Gretel pushed out the whole of one round window-pane, sat down, and enjoyed herself with it. Suddenly the door opened, and a very, very old woman, who supported herself on crutches, came creeping out. Hansel and Gretel were so terribly frightened that they let fall what they had in their hands. The old woman, however, nodded her head, and said, "Oh, you dear children, who has brought

you here? Do come in, and stay with me. No harm shall happen to you." She took them both by the hand, and led them into her little house. Then good food was set before them, milk and pancakes, with sugar, apples, and nuts. Afterwards two pretty little beds were covered with clean white linen, and Hansel and Gretel lay down in them, and thought they were in heaven.

The old woman had only pretended to be so kind; she was in reality a wicked witch, who lay in wait for children, and had only built the little house of bread in order to entice them there. When a child fell into her power, she killed it, cooked and ate it, and that was a feast day for her. Witches have red eyes, and cannot see far, but they have a keen scent like the beasts, and are aware when human  beings draw near. When Hansel and Gretel came into her neighbourhood, she laughed maliciously, and said mockingly, "I have them, they shall not escape me again!" Early in the morning before the children were awake, she was already up, and when she saw both of them sleeping and looking so pretty, with their plump red cheeks, she muttered to herself, "That will be a dainty mouthful!" Then she seized Hansel with her shrivelled hand, carried him into a little stable, and shut him in with a grated door.

He might scream as he liked, that was of no use. Then she went to Gretel, shook her till she awoke, and cried, "Get up, lazy thing, fetch some water, and cook something good for thy brother, he is in the stable outside, and is to be made fat. When he is fat, I will eat him." Gretel began to weep bitterly, but it was all in vain, she was forced to do what the wicked witch ordered her.

And now the best food was cooked for poor Hansel, but Gretel got nothing but crab-shells. Every morning the woman crept to the little stable, and cried, "Hansel, stretch out thy finger that I may feel if thou wilt soon be fat." Hansel, however, stretched out a little bone to her, and the old woman, who had dim eyes, could not see it, and thought it was Hansel's finger, and was astonished that there was no way of fattening him. When four weeks had gone by, and Hansel still continued thin, she was seized with impatience and would not wait any longer. "Hello, Gretel," she cried to the girl,"be active, and bring some water. Let Hansel be fat or lean, to-morrow I will kill him, and cook him." Ah, how the poor little sister did lament when she had to fetch the water, and how her tears did flow down over her cheeks! "Dear God, do help us," she cried. "If the wild beasts in the forest had but devoured us, we should at any rate have died together." "Just keep thy noise to thyself," said the old woman, "all that won't help thee at all."

Early in the morning, Gretel had to go out and hang up the cauldron with the water, and light the fire. "We will bake first," said the old woman, "I have already heated the oven, and kneaded the dough." She pushed poor Gretel out to the oven, from which flames of fire were already darting. "Creep in," said the witch,"and see if it is properly heated, so that we can shut the bread in."And when once Gretel was inside, she intended to shut the oven and let her bake in it, and then she would eat her, too. But Gretel saw what she had in her mind, and said, "I do not know how I am to do it; how do you get in?" "Silly goose," said the old woman, "The door is big enough; just look, I can get in myself!" and she crept up and thrust her head into the oven. Then Gretel gave her a push that drove her far into it, and shut the iron door, and fastened the bolt. Oh! then she began to howl quite horribly, but Gretel ran away, and the godless witch was miserably burnt to death.

Gretel, however, ran like lightning to Hansel, opened his little stable, and cried, "Hansel, we are saved! The old witch is dead!" Then Hansel sprang out like a bird from its cage when the door is opened for it. How they did rejoice and embrace each other, and dance about and kiss each other! And as they had no longer any need to fear her, they went into the witch's house, and in every corner there stood chests full of pearls and jewels. "These are far better than pebbles!" said Hansel, and thrust into his pockets whatever could be got in, and Gretel said, "I, too, will take something home with me," and filled her pinafore full. "But now we will go away." said Hansel, "that we may get out of the witch's forest."

When they had walked for two hours, they came to a great piece of water. "We cannot get over," said Hansel, "I see no foot-plank,and no bridge." "And no boat crosses either," answered Gretel, "but a white duck is swimming there; if I ask her, she will help us over." Then she cried,

"Little duck, little duck, dost thou see, Hansel and Gretel are waiting for thee? There's never a plank, or bridge in sight, take us across on thy back so white."

The duck came to them, and Hansel seated himself on its back, and told his sister to sit by him. "No," replied Gretel, "that will be too

heavy for the little duck; she shall take us across, one after the other."
The good little duck did so, and when they were once safely across
and had walked for a short time, the forest seemed to be more and
more familiar to them, and at length they saw from afar their father's
house. Then they began to run, rushed into the parlour, and threw
themselves into their father's arms. The man had not known one
happy hour since he had left the children in the forest; the woman,
however, was dead. Gretel emptied her pinafore until pearls and
precious stones ran about the room, and Hansel threw one handful
after another out of his pocket to add to them. Then all anxiety was
at an end, and they lived together in perfect happiness. My tale is
done, there runs a mouse, whosoever catches it, may make himself a
big fur cap out of it.

Mother Holle

There was once a widow who had two daughters—one of whom was pretty and industrious, whilst the other was ugly and idle. But she was much fonder of the ugly and idle one, because she was her own daughter; and the other, who was a step-daughter, was obliged to do all the work, and be the Cinderella of the house. Every day the poor girl had to sit by a well, in the highway, and spin and spin till her fingers bled.

Now it happened that one day the shuttle was marked with her blood, so she dipped it in the well, to wash the mark off; but it dropped out of her hand and fell to the bottom. She began to weep,and ran to her step-mother and told her of the mishap. But she scolded her sharply, and was so merciless as to say, "Since you have let the shuttle fall in, you must fetch it out again."

So the girl went back to the well, and did not know what to do; and in the sorrow of her heart she jumped into the well to get the shuttle. She lost her senses; and when she awoke and came to herself again, she was in a lovely meadow where the sun was shining and many thousands of flowers were growing. Along this meadow she went, and at last came to a baker's oven full of bread, and the bread cried out, "Oh, take me out! take me out! or I shall burn; I have been baked a long time!" So she went up to it, and took out all the loaves one after another with the bread-shovel. After that she went on till she came to a tree covered with apples, which called out to her, "Oh, shake me! shake me! we apples are all ripe!" So she shook the tree till the apples fell like rain, and went on shaking till they were all down, and when she had gathered them into a heap, she went on her way.

At last she came to a little house, out of which an old woman peeped; but she had such large teeth that the girl was frightened, and was about to run away.

But the old woman called out to her, "What are you afraid of, dear child? Stay with me; if you will do all the work in the house properly, you shall be the better for it. Only you must take care to make my bed well, and shake it thoroughly till the feathers fly—for then there is snow on the earth. I am Mother Holle.

As the old woman spoke so kindly to her, the girl took courage and agreed to enter her service. She attended to everything to the satisfaction of her mistress, and always shook her bed so vigorously that the feathers flew about like snow-flakes. So she had a pleasant life with her; never an angry word; and boiled or roast meat every day.

She stayed some time with Mother Holle, and then she became sad. At first she did not know what was the matter with her, but found at length that it was home-sickness: although she was many thousand times better off here than at home, still she had a longing to be there. At last she said to the old woman, "I have a longing for home; and however well off I am down here, I cannot stay any longer; I must go up again to my own people." Mother Holle said, "I am pleased that you long for your home again, and as you have served me so truly, I myself will take you up again." There upon she took her by the hand, and led her to a large door. The door was opened, and just as the maiden was standing beneath the doorway, a heavy shower of golden rain fell, and all the gold remained sticking to her, so that she was completely covered over with it.

"You shall have that because you have been so industrious," said Mother Holle, and at the same time she gave her back the shuttle which she had let fall into the well. Thereupon the door closed, and the maiden found herself up above upon the earth, not far from her mother's house.

And as she went into the yard the cock was standing by the well-side, and cried–

"Cock-a-doodle-doo! Your golden girl's come back to you!"

So she went in to her mother, and as she arrived thus covered with gold, she was well received, both by her and her sister.

The girl told all that had happened to her; and as soon as the mother heard how she had come by so much wealth, she was very anxious to obtain the same good luck for the ugly and lazy daughter. She had to seat herself by the well and spin; and in order that her shuttle might be stained with blood, she stuck her hand into a thorn bush and pricked her finger. Then she threw her shuttle into the well, and jumped in after it.

She came, like the other, to the beautiful meadow and walked along the very same path. When she got to the oven the bread again cried, "Oh, take me out! take me out! or I shall burn; I have been baked a long time!" But the lazy thing answered, "As if I had any wish to make myself dirty?" and on she went. Soon she came to the apple-tree, which cried, "Oh, shake me! shake me! we apples are all ripe!" But she answered, "I like that! one of you might fall on my head," and so went on.

When she came to Mother Holle's house she was not afraid, for she had already heard of her big teeth, and she hired herself to her immediately.

The first day she forced herself to work diligently, and obeyed Mother Holle when she told her to do anything, for she was thinking of all the gold that she would give her. But on the second day she began to be lazy, and on the third day still more so, and then she would not get up in the morning at all. Neither did she make Mother Holle's bed as she ought, and did not shake it so as to make the feathers fly up. Mother Holle was soon tired of this, and gave her notice to leave. The lazy girl was willing enough to go, and thought that now the golden rain would come. Mother Holle led her also to the great door; but while she was standing beneath it, instead of the gold a big kettle full of pitch was emptied over her. "That is the reward for your service," said Mother Holle, and shut the door.

So the lazy girl went home; but she was quite covered with pitch, and the cock by the well-side, as soon as he saw her, cried out–

"Cock-a-doodle-doo! Your pitchy girl's come back to you!"

But the pitch stuck fast to her, and could not be got off as long as she lived.

Important Hans Christian Andersen Stories for All Kids

THE EMPEROR'S NEW CLOTHES

Many years ago, there was an Emperor, who was so excessively fond of new clothes, that he spent all his money in dress. He did not trouble himself in the least about his soldiers; nor did he care to go either to the theatre or the chase, except for the opportunities then afforded him for displaying his new clothes. He had a different suit for each hour of the day; and as of any other king or emperor, one is accustomed to say, "he is sitting in council," it was always said of him, "The Emperor is sitting in his wardrobe."

Time passed merrily in the large town which was his capital; strangers arrived every day at the court. One day, two rogues, calling themselves weavers, made their appearance. They gave out that they knew how to weave stuffs of the most beautiful colours and elaborate patterns, the clothes manufactured from which should have the wonderful property of remaining invisible to everyone who was unfit for the office he held, or who was extraordinarily simple in character.

"These must, indeed, be splendid clothes!" thought the Emperor. "Had I such a suit, I might at once find out what men in my realms are unfit for their office, and also be able to distinguish the wise from the foolish! This stuff must be woven for me immediately." And he caused large sums of money to be given to both the weavers in order that they might begin their work directly.

So the two pretended weavers set up two looms, and affected to work very busily, though in reality they did nothing at all. They asked for the most delicate silk and the purest gold thread; put both into their own knapsacks; and then continued their pretended work at the empty looms until late at night.

"I should like to know how the weavers are getting on with my cloth," said the Emperor to himself, after some little time had elapsed; he was, however, rather embarrassed, when he remembered that a simpleton, or one unfit for his office, would be unable to see the manufacture. To be sure, he thought he had nothing to risk in his own person; but yet, he would prefer sending somebody else, to bring him intelligence about the weavers, and their work, before he troubled himself in the affair. All the people throughout the city had heard of the wonderful property the cloth was to possess; and all were anxious to learn how wise, or how ignorant, their neighbours might prove to be.

"I will send my faithful old minister to the weavers," said the Emperor at last, after some deliberation, "he will be best able to see how the cloth looks; for he is a man of sense, and no one can be more suitable for his office than he is."

So the faithful old minister went into the hall, where the knaves were working with all their might, at their empty looms. "What can be the meaning of this?" thought the old man, opening his eyes very wide. "I cannot discover the least bit of thread on the looms." However, he did not express his thoughts aloud.

The impostors requested him very courteously to be so good as to come nearer their looms; and then asked him whether the design pleased him, and whether the colours were not very beautiful; at the same time pointing to the empty frames. The poor old minister looked and looked, he could not discover anything on the looms, for a very good reason, viz: there was nothing there. "What!" thought he again. "Is it possible that I am a simpleton? I have never thought so myself; and no one must know it now if I am so. Can it be, that I am unfit for my office? No, that must not be said either. I will never confess that I could not see the stuff."

"Well, Sir Minister!" said one of the knaves, still pretending to work. "You do not say whether the stuff pleases you."

"Oh, it is excellent!" replied the old minister, looking at the loom through his spectacles. "This pattern, and the colours, yes, I will tell the Emperor without delay, how very beautiful I think them."

"We shall be much obliged to you," said the impostors, and then they named the different colours and described the pattern of the pretended stuff. The old minister listened attentively to their words, in order that he might repeat them to the Emperor; and then the knaves asked for more silk and gold, saying that it was necessary to complete what they had begun. However, they put all that was given them into their knapsacks; and continued to work with as much apparent diligence as before at their empty looms.

The Emperor now sent another officer of his court to see how the men were getting on, and to ascertain whether the cloth would soon be ready. It was just the same with this gentleman as with the minister; he surveyed the looms on all sides, but could see nothing at all but the empty frames.

"Does not the stuff appear as beautiful to you, as it did to my lord the minister?" asked the impostors of the Emperor's second ambassador; at the same time making the same gestures as before, and talking of the design and colours which were not there.

"I certainly am not stupid!" thought the messenger. "It must be, that I am not fit for my good, profitable office! That is very odd; however, no one shall know anything about it." And accordingly he praised the stuff he could not see, and declared that he was delighted with both colours and patterns. "Indeed, please your Imperial Majesty," said he to his sovereign when he returned, "the cloth which the weavers are preparing is extraordinarily magnificent."

The whole city was talking of the splendid cloth which the Emperor had ordered to be woven at his own expense.

And now the Emperor himself wished to see the costly manufacture, while it was still in the loom. Accompanied by a select number of officers of the court, among whom were the two honest men who had already admired the cloth, he went to the crafty impostors, who, as soon as they were aware of the Emperor's approach, went on working more diligently than ever; although they still did not pass a single thread through the looms.

"Is not the work absolutely magnificent?" said the two officers of the crown, already mentioned. "If your Majesty will only be pleased to look at it! What a splendid design! What glorious colours!" and at the same time they pointed to the empty frames; for they imagined that everyone else could see this exquisite piece of workmanship.

"How is this?" said the Emperor to himself. "I can see nothing! This is indeed a terrible affair! Am I a simpleton, or am I unfit to be an Emperor? That would be the worst thing that could happen–Oh! the cloth is charming," said he, aloud. "It has my complete approbation." And he smiled most graciously, and looked closely at the empty looms; for on no account would he say that he could not see what two of the officers of his court had praised so much. All his retinue now strained their eyes, hoping to discover something on the looms, but they could see no more than the others; nevertheless, they all exclaimed, "Oh, how beautiful!" and advised his majesty to have some new clothes made from this splendid material, for the approaching procession. "Magnificent! Charming! Excellent!" resounded on all sides; and everyone was uncommonly gay. The Emperor shared in the general satisfaction; and presented the impostors with the riband of an order of knighthood, to be worn in their button-holes, and the title of "Gentlemen Weavers."

The rogues sat up the whole of the night before the day on which the procession was to take place, and had sixteen lights burning, so that everyone might see how anxious they were to finish the Emperor's new suit. They pretended to roll the cloth off the looms; cut the air with their scissors; and sewed with needles without any thread in them. "See!" cried they, at last. "The Emperor's new clothes are ready!"

And now the Emperor, with all the grandees of his court, came to the weavers; and the rogues raised their arms, as if in the act of holding something up, saying, "Here are your Majesty's trousers! Here is the scarf! Here is the mantle! The whole suit is as light as a cobweb; one might fancy one has nothing at all on, when dressed in it; that, however, is the great virtue of this delicate cloth."

"Yes indeed!" said all the courtiers, although not one of them could see anything of this exquisite manufacture.

"If your Imperial Majesty will be graciously pleased to take off your clothes, we will fit on the new suit, in front of the looking glass."

The Emperor was accordingly undressed, and the rogues pretended to array him in his new suit; the Emperor turning round, from side to side, before the looking glass.

"How splendid his Majesty looks in his new clothes, and how well they fit!" everyone cried out. "What a design! What colours! These are indeed royal robes!"

"The canopy which is to be borne over your Majesty, in the procession, is waiting," announced the chief master of the ceremonies.

"I am quite ready," answered the Emperor. "Do my new clothes fit well?" asked he, turning himself round again before the looking glass, in order that he might appear to be examining his handsome suit.

The lords of the bedchamber, who were to carry his Majesty's train felt about on the ground, as if they were lifting up the ends of the mantle; and pretended to be carrying something; for they would by no means betray anything like simplicity, or unfitness for their office.

So now the Emperor walked under his high canopy in the midst of the procession, through the streets of his capital; and all the people standing by, and those at the windows, cried out, "Oh! How beautiful are our Emperor's new clothes! What a magnificent train there is to the mantle; and how gracefully the scarf hangs!" in short, no one would allow that he could not see these much-admired clothes; because, in doing so, he would have declared himself either a simpleton or unfit for his office. Certainly, none of the Emperor's various suits, had ever made so great an impression, as these invisible ones.

"But the Emperor has nothing at all on!" said a little child.

"Listen to the voice of innocence!" exclaimed his father; and what the child had said was whispered from one to another.

"But he has nothing at all on!" at last cried out all the people. The Emperor was vexed, for he knew that the people were right; but he thought the procession must go on now! And the lords of the bedchamber took greater pains than ever, to appear holding up a train, although, in reality, there was no train to hold.

THE LITTLE MATCH GIRL

Most terribly cold it was; it snowed, and was nearly quite dark, and evening–the last evening of the year. In this cold and darkness there went along the street a poor little girl, bareheaded, and with naked feet. When she left home she had slippers on, it is true; but what was the good of that? They were very large slippers, which her mother had hitherto worn; so large were they; and the poor little thing lost them as she scuffled away across the street, because of two carriages that rolled by dreadfully fast.

One slipper was nowhere to be found; the other had been laid hold of by an urchin, and off he ran with it; he thought it would do capitally for a cradle when he some day or other should have children himself. So the little maiden walked on with her tiny naked feet, that were quite red and blue from cold. She carried a quantity of matches in an old apron, and she held a bundle of them in her hand. Nobody had bought anything of her the whole livelong day; no one had given her a single farthing.

She crept along trembling with cold and hunger–a very picture of sorrow, the poor little thing!

The flakes of snow covered her long fair hair, which fell in beautiful curls around her neck; but of that, of course, she never once now thought. From all the windows the candles were gleaming, and it

smelt so deliciously of roast goose, for you know it was New Year's Eve; yes, of that she thought.

In a corner formed by two houses, of which one advanced more than the other, she seated herself down and cowered together. Her little feet she had drawn close up to her, but she grew colder and colder, and to go home she did not venture, for she had not sold any matches and could not bring a farthing of money: from her father she would certainly get blows, and at home it was cold too, for above her she had only the roof, through which the wind whistled, even though the largest cracks were stopped up with straw and rags.

Her little hands were almost numbed with cold. Oh! a match might afford her a world of comfort, if she only dared take a single one out of the bundle, draw it against the wall, and warm her fingers by it. She drew one out. "Rischt!" how it blazed, how it burnt! It was a warm, bright flame, like a candle, as she held her hands over it: it was a wonderful light. It seemed really to the little maiden as though she were sitting before a large iron stove, with burnished brass feet and a brass ornament at top. The fire burned with such blessed influence; it warmed so delightfully. The little girl had already stretched out her feet to warm them too; but–the small flame went out, the stove vanished: she had only the remains of the burnt-out match in her hand.

She rubbed another against the wall: it burned brightly, and where the light fell on the wall, there the wall became transparent like a veil, so that she could see into the room. On the table was spread a snow-white tablecloth; upon it was a splendid porcelain service, and the roast goose was steaming famously with its stuffing of apple and dried plums. And what was still more capital to behold was, the goose hopped down from the dish, reeled about on the floor with knife and fork in its breast, till it came up to the poor little girl; when– the match went out and nothing but the thick, cold, damp wall was left behind. She lighted another match. Now there she was sitting under the most magnificent Christmas tree: it was still larger, and more decorated than the one which she had seen through the glass door in the rich merchant's house.

Thousands of lights were burning on the green branches, and gaily-colored pictures, such as she had seen in the shop-windows, looked down upon her. The little maiden stretched out her hands towards them when–the match went out. The lights of the Christmas tree rose higher and higher, she saw them now as stars in heaven; one fell down and formed a long trail of fire.

"Someone is just dead!" said the little girl; for her old grandmother, the only person who had loved her, and who was now no more, had told her, that when a star falls, a soul ascends to God.

She drew another match against the wall: it was again light, and in the lustre there stood the old grandmother, so bright and radiant, so mild, and with such an expression of love.

"Grandmother!" cried the little one. "Oh, take me with you! You go away when the match burns out; you vanish like the warm stove, like the delicious roast goose, and like the magnificent Christmas tree!" And she rubbed the whole bundle of matches quickly against the wall, for she wanted to be quite sure of keeping her grandmother near her. And the matches gave such a brilliant light that it was brighter than at noon-day: never formerly had the grandmother been so beautiful and so tall. She took the little maiden, on her arm, and both flew in brightness and in joy so high, so very high, and then above was neither cold, nor hunger, nor anxiety–they were with God.

But in the corner, at the cold hour of dawn, sat the poor girl, with rosy cheeks and with a smiling mouth, leaning against the wall–frozen to death on the last evening of the old year. Stiff and stark sat the child there with her matches, of which one bundle had been burnt. "She wanted to warm herself," people said. No one had the slightest suspicion of what beautiful things she had seen; no one even dreamed of the splendour in which, with her grandmother she had entered on the joys of a new year.

Find out more about Krampus & his friends. Read some creepy stories or simply familiarise yourself with some fun facts behind the beast and the traditions/beliefs to do with folklore. Don't believe everything you hear or see about Krampus & similar beings. Read this book and make up your own mind.

Looking for stories that tell tales of bad, misbehaving, disobedient children or are you simply wanting stories that have important life lessons for children, then look no further. Here we have compiled famous German/Danish/Greek stories known well all over the world, that demonstrate/show what happens if/when children behave badly. All stories were written during a similar time frame (during the 1800's) either by the famous Brothers Grimm, Hans Christian Andersen, Aesop (a slave and storyteller who lived in ancient Greece between 620 and 564 B.C.), Wilhelm Busch & Dr. Heinrich Hoffman. Struwwelpeter has a collection of short stories, showing what happens to the children that misbehave, come up with mischievous ideas or simply don't pay attention to what they're doing. Whilst Max & Moritz is about two boys who pull pranks on everyone and pay the price themselves in the end. Even the Brothers Grimm and H. Andersen have some fairytales that explain to children the importance of teamwork, being careful, responsible and listening to one's parents. So go ahead read on what is contained in this book. We compiled this book with all the stories, because we believe that it is important that children learn life lessons contained in this book early on, we also believe that this is a must read for all parents.

www.ingramcontent.com/pod-product-compliance
Lightning Source LLC
Chambersburg PA
CBHW050402030726
47503CB00006B/1979